# My four-year-old
# the property investor

# My four-year-old
# the property
# investor

## The straight line to wealth

**Learn why many successful property
investors call this book their
lifelong guide to wealth building.**

# Cam McLellan
### with Matthew Lewison

Published by OpenCorp 2021
opencorp.com.au

First published 2012
Reprinted 2014, 2016, 2017, 2018, 2019, 2021

© 2011–2021 Cam McLellan
Written in collaboration with Matthew Lewison

 A catalogue record for this
book is available from the
National Library of Australia

ISBN: 9780646576534 (pbk)
ISBN: 9780992549442 (epub)

**Disclaimer**
While reasonable care has been taken to produce this guide, no guarantees are
given for the accuracy of its content or the material in the web links. Property
investing is a complex, ever-changing field. Every person's circumstance
is different, and therefore no reader should rely solely or partially on the
information in the guide or the material in web links provided by the author.
Any person or organisation reading this guide or obtaining material in the web
links is responsible for their own investment decisions. The OpenCorp group
of companies, its directors and employees are neither liable, nor responsible for
the result of any actions or losses incurred, whether whole or partial from the
use of the content, information or tools provided. The author is simply sharing
information he uses when investing.

Editor: Paul Hassing, thefeistyempire.com
Cover concept: damonza.com
Illustrations: Kim Fifield, fatfergusdesigns.com
Photography: ilonanelson.com
Typesetting: Helen Christie, bluewrenbooks.com.au

*For Angus, Ruby, Hannah and Lucy*

*Learn all the rules.*
*Then tear this world apart and build a better one.*

## Acknowledgements

There are many people I want to thank for their help and support in writing this book.

I assured **my wife Felicity** this would be a two-month project at most. I ended up writing night after night for well over a year. She reminded me a few times that I wasn't in fact married to my iPad. Felicity, thank you for your patience and your humble way.

The quality of this work is largely due to **Matt 'Lewie' Lewison.** Each month or so I'd hand Matt a pile of typewritten pages and not long after he'd return them decorated with his signature red pen. Most of the time it was simple grammatical corrections, but every so often I'd find a line through my work and PTO (please turn over) written beside it. Anyone who knows Matt will appreciate this. His finest contribution to this book is the 'developer's activity chain'. This diagram gives a fresh perspective on market movements that I know readers will find valuable. Matt, a massive thank-you from my family and me.

**Charlotte Newman** has the uncanny ability to decipher my handwriting even when I can't! She turned my drawn diagrams into professional, print-worthy illustrations for this book. Thank you so much for all your hard work.

**Gerard Ferrari,** the time you spent proofreading this work will always be appreciated. I applaud your passion for investing, business and, most importantly, family.

**Jonathan 'Hornet' Horn,** thanks for your painstaking work correcting my grammar. You are 'The Word Whisperer!'

**Michael 'Bozza' Beresford,** I told you a dozen times this would be the last time I needed my Excel formulas reconstructed. Keep living and breathing property!

**Steve Lewison,** thank you for your help and guidance when I was a rookie investor. You taught me the principles to succeed and kept me on the straight and narrow in the early days. You've never stopped reminding me that time is on my side.

Thanks for photographic mastery by **Ilona Nelson,** illustrations by **Kim Fifield** at Fat Fergus Design and cover concept by **Damonza.**

**Denise Mooney** and **Paul Hassing,** I can't thank you enough for fine-tuning my work. I look forward to working with you on many more projects.

**Palmer Higgs,** thank you for bringing it all together.

**Al Lewison,** I know you're not a hugger, so all I'll say is 'Cheers!'

My sincere thanks to you all.

## Foreword

Like all parents, Felicity and I encourage our kids to share. The one thing I ask, when you become an educated investor, is to share what you've learned with others.

The knowledge I've acquired over the years has been largely due to other investors kind enough to teach me the principles of success. Not one of these people asked for anything in return.

I've since developed a full understanding of the property market and the factors influencing it. This expertise has let me form a systematic investment strategy, which I've set out for you in this book.

I'd love to know your thoughts on what you read here. I'm always interested to hear stories, answer questions and discuss investment ideas and strategies.

Drop me a line at, cam@opencorp.com.au

I hope you enjoy reading this book as much as I enjoyed writing it.

# Contents

**Part 1**

# But why, Dad?

## But why, Dad?

I wrote this book for you, kids.

The idea came soon after our first daughter, Hannah, was born. Like many new dads, I had that moment of realisation: nothing else mattered except being a dad.

Soon after, I went for a medical. As I sat in the waiting room looking at all the sick people, I realised I was doing pretty well. But I also had a gut-wrenching thought: what if something happened to me?

Kids, you don't dwell on these things, but in case anything did happen, I felt responsible to pass on what I'd learned that I felt no one else could teach you.

This book is your guide to a life where everything's possible. If you follow this step-by-step investment plan, I know you won't have the financial worries I had in the early days.

This guide will help you build a portfolio of exceptional residential property; one that in time will give you passive cash flow *and* growth. I'll show you how to identify properties with strong rental yield and excellent growth potential, and how to use these investments as a platform to duplicate your portfolio. In this book I set out not just the basic knowledge and skills you need, but also the tools to help you keep everything in check.

I want to give you the means to choose your own adventure in life.

---

**'Dad, what's a portfolio?'** Kids, it's a collection of investments owned by individuals, a company or a trust. I'll explain trusts later.

---

**'What does yield mean Dad?'** Rental yield is money received as rent for a property. It's usually viewed as a percentage and compared to the property's cost.

**Rent = (weekly rent × 52 ÷ purchase price) × 100**
e.g. Rent = $450 per week. Purchase price = $450,000.
Yield = (450 × 52 ÷ 450,000) × 100 = 5.2%

---

**'Come on Dad; how long is it going to take?'** You can build a property portfolio that'll give you financial independence in 10–15 years.

---

That may sound like a long time, but consider this: 99% of the population are bound to a working level income for more than 45 years of their lives. I'm offering you a way to achieve financial freedom in a quarter of that time. This is starting to sound a lot better, isn't it?

## Dad's tips

- Kids, be patient. It takes time to build a property portfolio that'll give you financial freedom.
- Growth is the increase in value of your investments. Price growth is the key to building real wealth.

## Systems & overview or disorder & chaos

This is how I saw property investing when I began.

And this is how most people still see investing.

That's because they have neither a systematic approach, nor the tools to navigate the investment maze.

Kids, my goal with this book is to show you how to invest safely and successfully.

With the help of a clear overview and a proven system, this is how you'll see the investment 'maze'.

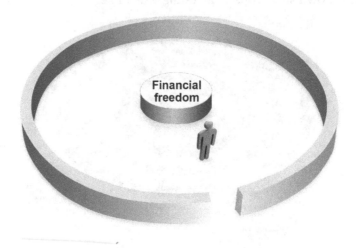

This is my gift to you.

Most parents tell their kids they can be anything in life. Sadly, most don't give them the tools to make this true.

As far as I can tell, we get only one chance at life. So don't hesitate to follow your dreams.

---

**Your only limit is your imagination.**

---

I'm 37, happily married to your mum and I have three of the most beautiful kids in the world.

Hannah, I never thought I could learn so many dance moves from a four-year-old! I still can't work out why you need seven clothes changes a day; but who am I to question. Sometimes I think you're already smarter than your dad. Negotiating with you is like tackling a university debate team! Hannah, you amaze me every day.

Angus, you're two-and-a-half and a true boy. Knees covered in Band-Aids from coming off your bike as you tear up the drive. While I'm not sure if it's climbing or jumping you love more; it seems the higher the better. If something has wheels and you can bash it, you're more than happy. Angus, I see myself every time I look at you.

Lucy, when I began this book you were three months old and had just started to smile when you saw me. Every dad knows how good that feels. Now, as I sit finishing this book, you're almost one and hanging on to the coffee table. Every now and then you let go and stand alone for a few seconds, beaming proudly. Lucy, like the other two kids your first word was 'Dad' which is all any dad wants to hear. I know, I might be soft, but don't tell anyone.

Kids, I want you to live life on your terms. Be who you want to be. Enjoy your profession, but don't let it define you (unless that's what you choose). Don't be afraid to try new things.

There's one vital thing if you want to build a portfolio. Make no mistake: you need to work hard. But the beauty of this is you can then fill your days doing what you *want*, not what you *must*, just to survive.

Before you can have a go at all your heart desires, you need to be one thing.

*A smart investor.*

---

**'What's a smart investor, Dad?'** Someone who actively invests in property with a clear vision and a refined system. Smart investors are *very* different to 'ordinary' investors.

---

To live a life where anything's possible, you need to build a property portfolio that'll give you substantial equity growth. Once we get your money issues solved, you can focus on enjoying life.

---

**'What's equity, Dad?'** Equity is the value of an asset, less the liability or loan held against it. It's the money you'd be left with if your asset was sold and the debt repaid.

---

## Dad's tips

- When you have a system, you minimise risk and stay in control.
- Risk minimisation is the key to safe investing.
- Live life kids. Your only limit is your imagination.

## Content overview

There's so much to learn about investing, but you don't need to know every detail to start. Part 2 gives a general appreciation of the investment world. If you follow the guide in Part 3, you'll learn as you go.

Take special note of the Table of contents because this book lays out a proven step-by-step system. If you follow each step in a straight line to Part 4 (Tools of the trade) you'll stay on track. I've also set out the content so you can easily refer back to the part you need later.

This book has four parts.

**Part 1**   An introduction to property investment, my story and how I started.

**Part 2**   The nuts and bolts of the industry. There's a lot to digest here. Consider this section your 'schooling'.

**Part 3**   The specifics of identifying solid, performing investments. I show you how I do this with a system I developed called 'the straight line to wealth'. I also show how to manage your portfolio and structure your investments using my 'circle of duplication'.

**Part 4**   I show you the tools to stay in control of your investment system. By aligning with each step of the straight line to wealth and the circle of duplication, these tools bring everything to life.

This part also features check sheets (for which I've provided a web link so you can see them full scale).

Here's a brief overview of the content again.

## Straight line of content

**Part 1**   But why, Dad?

**Part 2**   Kids, time for school

**Part 3**   The good stuff

**Part 4**   Tools of the trade

### Dad's tips

- There's a lot of information to learn about investing. You don't have to understand every detail before you start. Just ensure you follow a proven system.

## So, what does your dad do?

Kids, why should you believe anything your old man says? (Apart from the fact I'm the most fun guy in the world, of course!)

Outside our home, I'm a property investor.

Many people mistakenly think I can afford to invest in property because I'm a businessman. What they don't realise is that I built a property portfolio *first*.

Property investing *is* a business.

Your mum and I built our first portfolio of seven properties when she worked as a recruitment consultant and I was a telemarketer at Telstra. These were *not* high-paying jobs; back then I was on a base wage of $22k. The only reason I could afford to start my first business was that I had a property portfolio that gave me substantial usable equity.

Property investing is the safest form of wealth creation. It's less risky than running a business, and offers a far greater return on your time.

Aside from our investment portfolios, I own a funds management company specialising in syndicated property developments. We also provide education that assists with wealth creation for aspiring investors.

---

**'What's a development, Dad?'** Development is defined a number of ways. It can mean making a material change in the use of buildings or land (e.g. subdivision: breaking a large land parcel into smaller lots). It can also mean the construction of a building on land. Often it's both.

---

**'OK, so what's a funds management company?'** A funds management company (specialising in syndicated property development) sources funding from multiple investors, then manages the development process and risk for them.

---

After your Mum and I had built our first portfolio, I threw myself into business. Over the next fifteen years I built a group of companies that employs over 150 team members. These companies are listed in two *BRW (Business Review Weekly) fast starter* lists and six are in the *BRW fast 100.*

Your Uncle Al and I built and sold Australia's largest Telstra business centre. We also built and sold a company that specialised in IT support for medium sized businesses. While these were both very successful businesses life's too short, so we decided to focus on what we enjoyed: property.

Our Telstra business centre was my apprenticeship in building and strategically managing a medium-sized organisation. At first it was way tougher than I'd ever imagined. We started in an office half the size of your bedroom. My little brother Bob had just moved from the country and needed a job. He answered his first call with, 'G'day; s'goin'?'

After Bob had done some training, I went on the road selling, leaving him to handle the phones and fill mobile phone orders. We kept it simple. Our stock cupboard was the bottom drawer of a filing cabinet. Our next employee, your uncle Azza, had to stand to use his computer which sat on the filing cabinet as there was no room for another chair!

Sound fun? At times, the early years were far from fun. While we grew rapidly, we almost closed the doors four times: literally having to decide if we could afford to return to work the next day. When we did, we had to make sure we had smiles on our faces for the sake of our staff and customers.

Though I was very successful at sales, I had no experience of controlling a business, particularly cash flow and measured growth. I had to learn the hard way.

The only reason our business survived was that we had a substantial amount of money behind us. We sold most of the property portfolio to survive. Without it, our business would've been just another statistic.

Thankfully, even as I started selling what we owned from under her, your mum never lost faith in me.

The next business Al and I built was voted one of Australia's fastest-growing IT infrastructure servicing companies. Al spent time in the United States reviewing how the best IT firms ran. We picked different models apart and then built the systems that formed our business operation.

I spent my teens in Bairnsdale, Victoria. Sadly, I didn't see the value of school then. I was more concerned with the differences between Bon Scott and Brian Johnson. Not studying cost me a fortune, as I've had to employ people smarter than I to help with the basics I should've learned at school. Stay at school and study hard, kids: it'll make life *much* easier later on!

Your mum taught me to double-click a mouse at 23. I think it's funny I'd built one of Australia's fastest growing IT companies by 37.

I'm also a founder of OpenCorp (opencorp.com.au), an investment advisory, funds management and property development company. Your Uncle Al, with his brother Matt and their father Steve, are the other major shareholders.

Steve gave us our passion for bricks and mortar. In the early days, he pointed us in the right direction, showed us how to put the basics into practice and explained that property growth is the key to wealth creation.

Steve helped me through my first property purchase and guided me when I developed a unit in the backyard. I laugh now, but I had no idea. Steve even covered the first progress draw on my building contract as I couldn't get the finance. I was very lucky to have someone I trusted to help me start.

---

**'Dad, what's a progress draw?'** It's a payment made to a builder at each construction stage.

---

OpenCorp's concept business plan was Matt's brainchild. He has a double degree in civil engineering and corporate finance. Before OpenCorp, Matt was the Queensland General Manager for one of Australia's largest land development firms. Controlling over a billion dollars of development is impressive, especially for a guy in his 20s. But what's more important is the knowledge and systems you need to stay in control at this level.

Matt's skills complement Al's and mine very well. Apart from the advantage of working with mates, we're a well-rounded executive team.

We provide two distinct services:

- Property investment advisory and ongoing mentoring.
- Funds management through property development and property trusts.

We teach people how to build and manage a residential property portfolio. We guide clients throughout this process. Assisting with finance; our research team helps find and secure the property, we then ensure clients obtain suitable tenants. We then mentor clients on how to leverage their equity and duplicate the process to buy further investments.

It's a good feeling to watch people build wealth through property investment.

Our Fund Management Division's initial focus was to give Australians the chance to invest in well-managed development projects.

At time of writing, our 26 development project funds have provided average annualised investor returns of more than 18%.

The issue with our development funds was that we had too many investors and not enough developments that we deemed suitable to buy.

Also, while property development can deliver huge profits, it carries a fair amount of risk. Though some projects far outperformed our forecasts, others didn't deliver the profit we'd hoped to achieve for our clients.

We wanted to provide investors with more stable, income-based returns similar to our own property portfolios. So, after years of planning, we structured a new fund for investors called ResiFund (resifund.com.au).

ResiFund lets clients benefit not only from development profits but also the long-term rental and price growth of Australian residential property. This build-to-rent fund lets investors get into the property market with as little as $1k.

ResiFund is the first of its kind in Australia. We plan to eventually list it on the ASX so investors can trade their shares and enjoy the extra advantage of liquidity.

OpenCorp is a public company with an Australian Financial Services License (AFSL). This lets us create and operate Australian Securities and Investments Commission (ASIC) registered managed investment schemes for sophisticated and unsophisticated investors.

---

**'Dad, what's the difference between a sophisticated and an unsophisticated investor?'** Sophisticated investors are deemed to have enough knowledge to make informed decisions. They hold net assets of $2.5m or more or have a gross annual income (for each of the last two financial years) of $250k or more.

---

Some investment opportunities are available to sophisticated investors only.

---

**'What's leverage, Dad?'** Leverage is using other people's money (OPM) to give you a far greater return than you'd make on your own. I'll tell you more about it later.

---

Before founding OpenCorp, Steve, Matt, Al and I had shifted our focus from Melbourne and were investing mainly in a Brisbane infill area. Like other areas where we now invest, this suburb had good infrastructure and growth potential. We took it in turns to buy whenever land was released as the developer drip-feeding land to the market.

---

**'What's an infill area?'** It's vacant land surrounded by established housing. The great thing about an infill area is that once all the land is sold, the demand pressure usually causes prices to rise.

---

**'What's drip-feeding, Dad?'** It's a strategy large land developers use. They release blocks of land slowly to the market to ensure there's never enough supply to meet demand. This keeps upward pressure on prices.

---

We'd been investing and developing for many years by this stage. Our investment strategy was to build and hold three and four-bedroom spec homes with great growth potential, good rental yield and low vacancy rates. I'll explain more about why we did that later, but basically it was a case of the right city, the right area and the right home to build for that area.

---

**'Dad, what's a spec home?'** It's a home built by a developer who has designed it by speculating on the type of buyer or tenant who'd like to occupy the home, rather than building it to a specific customer order.

---

It took us years to develop the business model we now have at OpenCorp. Among our different groups, we have an acquisitions team that constantly researches each city market identifying worthy investment opportunities.

It's a great business, and very satisfying, as we're helping people build wealth. I tell our staff they're crazy if they're still working for me in 15 years. I'm very proud to say that many have already built impressive portfolios.

## Dad's tips

- Investing in property is the safest and most guaranteed form of wealth creation.
- It's important to have someone you trust to guide you in the early days.

## What do you really want?

Kids, to succeed as a property investor, you need a vision. A vision isn't just having a goal. It's a time, place and an environment in the future that you wish to create. A vision is much more powerful than a goal. I'm not saying you have to sit around like a monk, meditating and focusing on your vision. You must, however, be clear on what your desired personal and financial situation is. But remember, getting there is most of the fun.

In business, the prime measure of success is money.

Yet money isn't my vision. My vision is what I have now. Watching my family grow in an environment I've created.

In business, I invest in two things: people and processes.

For you to build wealth through property investing, the same applies, except:

People = you. Process = this book.

It's that simple.

### Dad's tips

- What environment do you wish to create for yourself in the future?
- You must be clear on your desired situation.
- Getting there is most of the fun!

## Money fears

Kids, let's talk about fear and money.

You might hear people say money is 'evil'. But anyone who says that doesn't have any! When you have money, you have the power to make the world a better place. What could be evil about that? The old saying 'money can't buy happiness' should end with 'it won't make you sad either'.

Money gives you choice and lets you do what you want. Be careful, though; don't waste money or flash it in people's faces.

Above all, be humble.

This reminds me of a story about Kerry Packer (then Australia's richest man). He was in a Las Vegas casino when he heard a guy mouthing off about how he was worth $60m.

After a while, Packer turned to the guy and said, 'I'll flip you for it; double or nothing.'

The lesson? There's *always* someone bigger and badder than you.

### Dad's tips

- Money can't buy happiness, but it won't make you sad. Don't throw money around or flash it in friends' faces.
- Always be humble.

## Time: tick tick ...

What does money give me? Precious time. I now wake (actually, Angus wakes me) at around 6am. I get his brekkie, then run to CrossFit while listening to some tunes. I get to the office at around 10am, have meeting after meeting, then leave around 3pm.

What property investing and money give me is time with family. And that's all that matters to me.

I once heard a saying: 'To a child, love is spelt T-I-M-E'. So I'll play with you as much as possible now, because I know that once you hit your teens, Dad won't be quite so cool. I'll then leave raising you to the future Lady Gaga. (You know what I mean!)

## Dad's tips

- Property investment and money give you time for the important things in life.

# What is financial freedom?

Even as a kid, retiring at 40 was my vision. For me, this was the definition of financial freedom. I pictured a never-ending adventure holiday of extreme sports around the world. I'm now 37 with an entirely different view of financial freedom. You little spew-monkeys changed all that. (Unless trampolining is considered an extreme sport!)

I want you to realise the importance of working hard when you have to.

At 8 years of age I started work delivering newspapers. At 14 my mum said, 'Welcome to the real world! You're paying board and buying your own clothes now, so you need to start earning'.

My work life began at the *Bairnsdale Advertiser* putting papers together. I've been a supermarket fruit-and-veg manager and then store manager. I've stacked more shelves than I care to remember. I've pumped petrol, scooped ice cream and flipped burgers. I've hung off the back of a garbage truck (when bins used to be emptied by hand). I once fell asleep standing on the back and lost a fair bit of bark as I rolled down the road. I've been a plumber's assistant. I've picked paddocks of gherkins and broccoli and stacked thousands of mud bricks. I've sorted recycling at a tip (the worst job). I've also baled hay, driven backhoes and even crashed a few forklifts.

I did all this before 18. For years I held two or three jobs at a time and I've had many more since. I left home at 17 and did what I needed to make a dollar and survive. I worked my backside off in every job I held. I made sure I did more than the next person and I always looked for ways to make improvements.

Kids, I used to carry my horse through the snow – to work and back!

But I feel I've been rewarded in the long term.

My brothers have the same work ethic. Andy's a builder and the hardest worker I know. He spent years on oil rigs and is now in mining. Bob's one of the best salespeople you'll find. He holds several national sales records in the telecommunications industry. Both have now built impressive property portfolios. Maybe my mum's hard-line approach to the real world is the right way to go, kids. It certainly hardened us up.

Though I worked hard, I hated being tied to a job, with my future controlled by someone else. I felt trapped. But once I started investing, I actually enjoyed my employment years. I was there because I wanted to be. My investment properties gave me a large degree of satisfaction. The main thing I wanted was to break the financial shackles that society puts on us all.

Like many others who dream of financial freedom, I saw life mapped out and felt locked in an endless cycle of bad debt. Society programs us to follow a cookie-cutter life model. Go to school. Get a job. Buy a house (with a 25-year mortgage). Have a family (which is great, but it locks you in even more). Then grind away at that mortgage.

Kids, this is normal life for most Australians. But it freaked me out.

Don't get me wrong; I love the Aussie lifestyle. And I love being part of society (just not financially). It means you kids grow up in a stable environment with good people around you.

So what is financial freedom? It means *everything's* possible.

As soon as Richard Branson gets his rocket off the ground, I'll buy a ticket to outer space. I've dreamed of looking back at Earth since I saw *Star Wars* when I was five.

Property investing is my ticket to making things happen.

## Dad's tips

- Work harder than those around you and opportunities will come your way. Always look at areas for improvement.
- Be prepared to work hard in a job. You needn't earn huge dollars. But the more you earn, the faster you can build your portfolio.
- Investing lets you do *what* you want, *when* you want.
- Financial freedom means everything's possible.
- Always appreciate the Aussie way of life.

# Part 2

# Kids, time for school

## How much income is enough, Dad?

So how much annual income do you need to be financially independent?

It's not just a question of how *much* you'll need, but also how *long* you'll need it. As the graph shows, we're living longer and spending more time in retirement, which means we need more money to fund it. And because we're spending longer in education before entering the workforce, we need to accumulate wealth at a much faster rate.

I know retirement sounds a long way off to you kids, but you can't stop the clock!

## Time spent

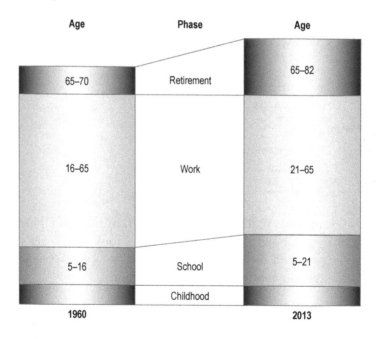

That's why I advise you to build a property portfolio that'll grow in value and increase in rental yield faster than the Consumer Price Index (CPI). As long as you stay healthy, you'll have enough income to live very comfortably in retirement. Over time, your passive income and equity will grow much larger than the holding costs of your portfolio.

I'll go over some figures for you later.

---

**'What's CPI, Dad?'** The Consumer Price Index measures the change in prices paid by households (consumers) for goods and services over time.

---

Now, all you need to figure out is how much annual income you'll need.

Let's start with a question.

In today's money, how much would you need to fund your desired lifestyle?

Let's look at your current budget, Hannah.

| Lollies | $3 |
|---------|----|
| Toy | $20 |
| DVD | $15 |
| Nails | $5 |

It all adds up, doesn't it? But a girl should enjoy the good things in life. I'd never seen you happier than when I took you to get your fingernails painted for the first time. But you looked even more amused after you made me get mine painted too.

The thing is, when you eventually leave home, living expenses may add up to more than you think. And if you're anything like me, you'll enjoy playing with big-kid toys that cost serious money.

In today's money, $150k per year of passive income is a good start. According to the Australian Bureau of Statistics (ABS), today's average annual salary is about $69k.

So when do you need to start earning this amount?

Most people would say right now. But most people aren't prepared to stick to a plan and wait for the rewards. Others hesitate or get sidetracked and miss their chance.

We'll examine how best to achieve financial freedom, and the likely time frames, but I want to cover some other points first.

## Dad's tips

- In today's dollars, how much do you need to fund your desired lifestyle?
- Less time in the workforce means you must accumulate wealth at a much faster rate if you want a carefree retirement.
- Be prepared to stick to a plan and wait for the rewards.

## Kick to kick

Kids, find someone to play kick to kick. Investing is fun, but it's even more fun when you share your passion for wealth building with someone else. Be it your wife, husband, brother or sister (or even your dear old dad), it's priceless to have someone to motivate and keep you on track, bounce ideas off and give you a reality check when the bright lights dazzle. Because all that glitters in the investment world is *not* gold!

Your mum and I often talk property but it's not her passion. My teammate throughout my property journey has been your Uncle Al. Our initial learning curve was ferocious. We absorbed information from every source and kicked ideas back and forth. With the information we acquired, we built an arsenal of knowledge and developed our strategy which is what this book will teach you.

Kids, property investing is a skill that can be learned. When my personal trainer bought another property with his wife, he asked how I'd acquired so much investment expertise. I explained that property investing is like any other profession. As a personal trainer, he studied anatomy, diet and exercise before putting it all into practice at the gym. He knows the actions needed to achieve specific results. Property investing is the same.

Most investors learn from other investors, fine-tuning their strategy as they start doing it themselves.

Consider your education a work in progress and remember it's important to keep moving ahead. With property investing, getting started is the most important part.

I'm still learning and I always will be.

### Dad's tips

- It's much more fun to share your passion for investing.
- Follow a proven strategy and stick to it.
- Property investing is a skill that can be learned like any other. Learn from other investors.
- Education never stops.

My four-year-old the property investor

# Why did I choose property?

Why did I start investing in property?

Because I wanted a wealth-building strategy that provided an excellent return for a reasonably low risk.

My dad quoted a statistic when I was eight and I've never forgotten it.

---

**'Ninety percent of all millionaires become so through owning real estate.'** Andrew Carnegie – Industrialist, philanthropist and *very* rich self-made man.

---

While this statistic is reducing due to fortunes being made through technology, it's still true today.

'Old money' is wealth that's been passed down through generations. In almost every case I've studied, old money has the same foundation.

## Land

The British royal family is an ideal example. They amassed huge wealth simply by owning all the land and collecting rent from everyone who lived on it.

Smart investors know that if you want to assess an investment opportunity, you must consider a risk vs return ratio. The following table is a standard risk matrix.

## Risk matrix

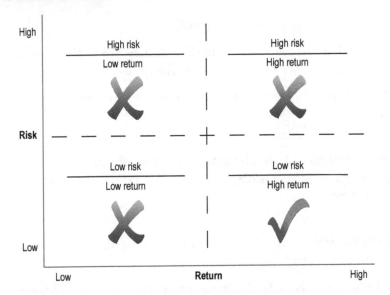

Unfortunately, most investment opportunities fall in the low risk/ low return or high risk/high return quadrants. This doesn't mean you don't consider them. It just means you need to do your research and understand the risk so you can manage it properly.

Before we compare property risk and return to other investment vehicles, I want to talk basics.

When selecting an investment property, the first step is to assess each city market. Next you choose the appropriate area in that market. Only then do you look at the property.

**Market – Area – Property**

Choose the city market with the best potential for growth.

Determine the best area that'll provide a good balance of yield and growth.

Select the optimum size and quality investment property for that area.

I'll go into more detail about this process later.

First, let's talk about market history. It's really important to factor in historic movements when you're identifying potential investments. History is the first thing we look at when choosing a market. This graph shows how median house prices have tracked over the last 40 years.

---

**'Dad, what's the median house price?'** The median is the middle price in a series of sales. For example, if nine sales in an area are ordered from highest to lowest in value, the fifth sale price is the median. Don't confuse the median price with the average sale price (mean or medium). This is a common mistake.

---

## Median house price—Graph A

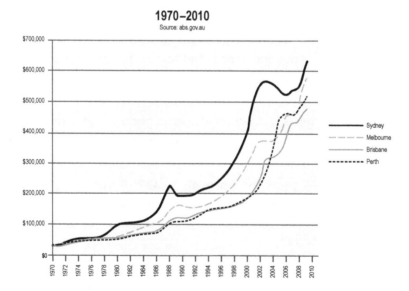

**1970–2010**
Source: abs.gov.au

If you look at Graph A, you'll see that Melbourne tracks behind Sydney. I tend to use Sydney as a lead market indicator. The Sydney and Melbourne property markets are primarily driven by the business economy. But Sydney has a stronger business economy so generally the Sydney property market lifts before Melbourne's. So I watch and once the Sydney market starts to lift

I check a number of other factors that we will go over later and if all looks good, I start buying in Melbourne. Perth and Brisbane move independently as their main industry drivers are tourism and mining.

In case you're wondering, I limit my investing to the four major capital cities. I'll explain why later.

There are other important factors to consider when choosing investments. By analysing all this information, you'll minimise risk and improve your chances of investing just before a market upswing.

---

**'Dad, where can I find this information?'** abs.gov.au is a good starting point. It's not fun to navigate but it has valuable data. Watch out for stats and charts that relate to your chosen markets.

---

In terms of the amount of data you need to study, go for 40 years or more. This lets you spot trends and understand average growth over time. You can also see yearly spikes and dips and consider what economics may have caused them.

A feature of Graph A is the dramatic rise in prices towards the end. This shows the compounding growth of property values over time.

---

**'Dad, what does compound growth mean?'** Growth on growth. Try this exercise to help you understand compound growth. If you had 1 cent and doubled it every day for 30 days, what would the end amount of money be?

---

The graph also shows that markets get knocked around from time to time. Look what happened in 1987 (after the stock market crash). People ditched shares to invest in property. As a result, property prices rose. In the early 1990s recession, interest rates hit 17%. Property prices dived until the economy settled as people realised the world wasn't ending.

My four-year-old the property investor

Kids, looking at Graph A, let me ask you this. If you'd bought a property in 1989, would you have been happy with your purchase in 1992? In most cities you'd say no. But remember, the key to building wealth is to buy as soon as you can afford it and hold for the long term.

Now a different question. If you bought a property in 1989 and still held it today, would you be happy? Of course you would. You'd be stoked! While stats are a good source of historical information, it's important you don't get 'analysis paralysis'. Stick to my selection criteria outlined in Part 3; buy and hold for the long term.

This next graph factors in average growth over the last 50 years of 8.7% (source: ABS). I've then carried that 8.7% forward for another 50 years.

## Median house price—Graph B

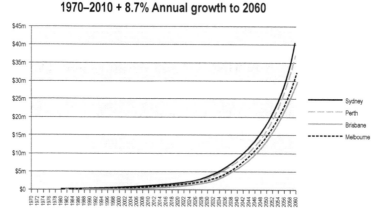

1970–2010 + 8.7% Annual growth to 2060

Can you imagine that in 50 years, a standard house will be worth $40m? It seems ridiculous. Yet I'm sure people who bought a house for $15k 50 years ago never imagined it'd be worth $500k today. Just 30 years ago, being a millionaire was an impressive feat. Now it's not such a huge deal. That's due to the ever-decreasing value of cash in the economy.

Let's look at other factors that help us determine future growth.

It's useful to understand the foundations of long-term appreciation:

- The Australian population is growing faster than ever, with growth of 394,000 people in 2012 alone.

- The National Housing Supply Council (a government body established to monitor the housing shortage) estimates we have an undersupply of 228,000 homes at time of writing.

- The Council forecasts this number to exceed 663,600 by 2031. That's *four times* the number of homes Australia builds in a *year*! This is the opposite of the current situation in the US where they have a housing oversupply.

- Capital city residential vacancy rates are low and demand for rental property remains exceptionally strong.

- Australia is one of the world's best performing economies, and we're earning more than ever.

These figures don't mean we'll have 640,600 homeless people by 2029. The forecast factors vacancy rates, social housing and other variables.

This information is valuable, but you should be discerning. Ask yourself who compiled it and what their agenda may be.

That said, these figures clearly show Australia faces a chronic undersupply of affordable housing. For an investor, that's a good thing.

## Dad's tips

- Over 90% of the world's millionaires made their first million from property.
- Investing in growth property is like a bad haircut. Time fixes everything.
- Realising capital appreciation on your properties is your foundation for building wealth.

My four-year-old the property investor

## Leverage & other people's money (OPM)

So what the heck is leverage? Kids, I want you to think of the see-saw in our local park. You little tackers are pretty strong. You tried to lift me off the ground many times, but I was just too heavy. Then you figured out that, when you all sat on the end of the see-saw opposite me, you could easily *lever* me into the air.

**The power of leverage lets you achieve great effect with minimal force.**

This is what happens when you invest using other people's money (OPM). You make a far greater return than you would have on your own. We'll discuss banks and financial structures later.

First, get used to the terms.

Leverage and OPM. In other words, debt.

You must understand the power of leveraging OPM to seriously accelerate your portfolio's growth. By adding OPM to your own money when you invest, you get a much greater result when a price rise occurs.

What I'm saying is, never be scared of *good* debt.

To show how this works, let's say Angus and Lucy both have $1.

They go the shops to buy an apple each. (What good kids, sticking to the fruit; Mum will be pleased!)

In the shop, an apple costs $1, but an apple *seed* costs $5.

Angus, like his dad, wants his apple right now.

But Lucy thinks for a moment. Instead of buying her apple right away, she goes home and asks Hannah for a loan of $4 (OPM) which she promises to repay with ten apples at a later date.

Lucy buys and plants the seed. At first it grows very slowly. But after a few years, this single tree starts to produce more apples than Lucy thought possible. She uses the seeds from these new apples to plant more and more trees.

From that one seed, Lucy is able to repay Hannah the apples she owed *and* grow enough apple trees to last a lifetime (and beyond). All because she used OPM to leverage her investment and increase her returns.

Kids, learn to love and understand numbers. If you know numbers, and how banks work, you can really make money work for you.

A vital rule to remember is that you succeed only if you invest in *appreciating* assets. Using OPM to buy toys or fund your lifestyle is very dangerous and can set you back years.

### Dad's tips

- Leveraging is using other people's money (OPM) to make a far greater return than you would have on your own.
- Using OPM to buy toys or fund your lifestyle is very dangerous.

## Duplication: 1 + 1 = 5

Once you've learned to identify good investments, the key to portfolio growth is quickly identifying when your usable equity has increased. Banks will convert this usable equity to cash, which you can deposit on further investments.

This is called duplication.

---

**'Why is it important to understand duplication, Dad?'** Kids, duplicating an effective investment system is very important. If you keep buying good investments, duplication helps you grow wealth. However, duplication without a *system* only compounds risk.

---

It's vital to have a system that lets you monitor the market for movement. If you spot a price rise, you need to revalue your portfolio, increase your line of credit (also called contingent liability) and unlock your usable equity. *Then* it's time to duplicate.

Part 3 explains the process of identifying worthy investments. I also show how to effectively manage your investments so you can use your equity as a platform to keep duplicating your portfolio.

Available equity that's not being used is called *lazy* equity. If you're growing a property portfolio, lazy equity is one of the biggest (and most common) mistakes you can make.

---

**'How can equity be lazy, Dad?'** Equity that's at your disposal but not being used is lazy. To supercharge your investment strategy, use your available equity for deposits on additional investments.

---

Every day lazy equity sits idle, you miss opportunities to duplicate and move closer to financial freedom.

This diagram shows how to duplicate a portfolio by using an equity increase in one property to put a deposit on another. This means you needn't keep saving for each deposit. Now, imagine you have several properties that go through a growth cycle. This large equity increase means your ability to duplicate is compounded.

## Property 1 buys Property 2

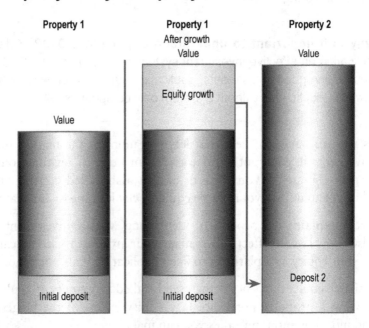

Remember how Lucy used that single seed to grow all those apple trees? Imagine if she'd used *two* seeds in the first year. She'd have doubled her results, letting her plant twice as much the following year, and so on.

My four-year-old the property investor

The same thing happens with property duplication. The more asset value you have in your portfolio when a price rise occurs, the more substantial your equity platform becomes. You can use this equity to buy again, duplicating your portfolio each time. This is called the 'compounding effect'. You'll notice it when you have multiple properties that go through a growth period at the same time. When this happens, let the good times roll!

The key to successful investing is to enter the market as soon as possible and duplicate when you have usable equity. As you use equity in your investments, take time to invest in your education. It'll help you avoid costly mistakes. According to the Australian Taxation Office (ATO), only around 15,280 Australians own more than six properties. Given the millions of properties in Australia, these relatively few people must own a lot more than six properties each. The rich get richer while everyone else does the same old thing.

The good news is that investing isn't so hard once you start.

---

**'So, Dad, if you use equity growth for new deposits, how much does it cost to hold all these properties?'** Kids, that's a good question; I'll discuss holding costs later. But before we consider the cost of investing, what's the cost of *not* investing?

---

You don't have to own a suburb to achieve financial independence. A handful of smart investments is enough.

Consider a scenario of five very conservative properties bought over 12 years. Note the growth to the 20-year mark, even if you stop buying property well before then.

Note that factors such as capital growth, rental yields and wages seldom rise at the same rate each year. Over 10 to 20 years you can expect variations, but the examples below make reasonable assumptions for this exercise.

Assumptions

- $90k annual average household income with a 5% annual wage rise.

- First property bought at $400k.

- On average 8% annual property value increase.

- Rental yield of 4.5% of the property's value.

- 7% interest rate.

Kids, I want you to understand something about building wealth. What matters isn't so much the *number* of properties you accumulate, as the *net wealth* you build over time. This example shows what you can do with five properties bought over 12 years – a very realistic achievement for most investors.

## 5 homes in 12 years

### Net wealth over time against holding cost

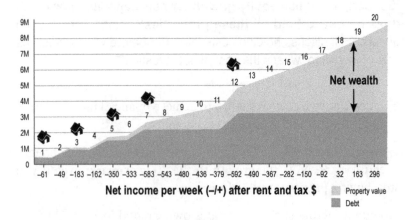

My four-year-old the property investor

The graph shows the year each property was bought, total portfolio value, net wealth, accumulated debt and weekly holding costs.

For the first five or six years, you'll see that wealth builds very slowly. But as the properties grow in value, net wealth compounds to climb at a much faster rate. Debt levels stay the same after year 12, when the final property has been acquired.

At the bottom of the graph, I've noted net income (-/+) after rent and tax. I haven't sugar-coated these figures. You'll see that during years 11 to 13, weekly holding costs peak at around $100 per property.

That's around $32k net per year; a large amount to fund with earned income. But that's not our plan because during these years, average net wealth is rising at a much faster rate than holding costs.

You can access this equity by refinancing and creating a line of credit to cover holding costs. It's likely you'll need to keep using these funds until the rent covers the holding costs. This is standard practice for many investors.

By making this line of credit available, you can cover loss of income for weeks between tenants as well as repairs and maintenance costs. In this way, you can still have a reasonable lifestyle while building your wealth.

Check the graph again to see how much net wealth has grown by year 15. The results may seem dramatic but, as the famous physicist Albert Einstein said,

---

**'Compounding is the eighth wonder of the world. He who understands it, earns it. He who doesn't, pays it.'**

---

The amount of net wealth at year 15 is around $2.8m while the total value is about $5.9m. Now, kids, think back to our passive income target of $150k per year. If you factor an 8% growth rate onto your $5.9m property portfolio, this equity growth will give you $470k to live on per year!

It's important to realise growth won't occur evenly each year, but when you experience a growth period on a number of properties, work becomes a *choice* not a necessity.

Five properties in 12 years is a very conservative investment approach. But I want you to know this is all you need for a comfortable life.

Another achievable aim is to build a portfolio of 10 properties in 10 years. I've seen many people do it, though you need higher personal income to pay initial holding costs.

The key is to build momentum so that by years 8, 9 and 10, you can buy two properties a year. That may sound a lot, but if four of your properties rise in value, buying several more at a time is easy. You may buy one property in the first year and none for several years. Then you may buy two, three or more properties in a single year.

To do this, you must follow a system that lets you accurately and regularly monitor the market. I recommend a check every three to six months. When your usable equity increases, act fast and buy again. Then, when you've bought all the property your usable equity will allow, sit back, enjoy life and wait for another market rise.

The property review checklist provided in the tools section will help you monitor market sale prices and rental yields.

## Dad's tips

- Banks will convert usable equity into cash you can use for deposits on further investments. This is called duplication.
- Usable equity that's not put to use is called lazy equity.
- The more property value you hold in your portfolio when a price rise occurs, the more equity you can use to buy more property and duplicate your portfolio. This is called the compounding effect.
- Enter the market as soon as possible and duplicate when you have enough usable equity.

# Exit strategy: begin with the end in mind

You should start by picturing your desired outcome. Remember your vision for the future. Otherwise, it's easy to get distracted and stray from the systematic investment path. I list four main exit strategies for property investors below. Consider your initial setup and holding structure, as this will impact your exit strategy timing.

1. **Sell to pay debt.** There are pros and cons to this strategy. Many people wish to be debt free and their sole financial goal is to pay off the family home.

   Kids, from time to time you'll hear the saying 'work smarter, not harder'. But most people don't do this. Instead, they work hard to pay off the family home with income they earn from a job. And that's a big waste of time.

   I realise most people have been conditioned to think this way by parents and society. But that doesn't make it a viable strategy. Here's an example that shows why paying off the family home over 25 to 30 years with earned income is a bad strategy.

   Let's say you buy just three properties in your life: two well-chosen investment properties and a family home.

   For simplicity, we'll say each property cost $500k and the total loan is $1.5m. Tax breaks and rental income will help you fund most loan repayments.

| Investment property value | $1.0m |
|---|---|
| Family home value | $500k |
| Total property value | $1.5m |

As we know, well-chosen property doubles in value about every 7 to 10 years. Given this, all you need do to become debt free is hold the investment properties through one full growth cycle, then sell them.

This means your two investment properties will double in value from $1m to $2m during the cycle. If you sell them at this point for $2m, you incur 25% capital gains tax (CGT) on the profit (not 50%, as you held the properties for more than a year). The remaining amount is $1.75m.

You can now repay the $1.5m debt on the investment properties and your home, leaving you with $250k to play with. I'm sure you'll think of something to do with the extra money!

This is a simple example of what you can do, though it's not the strategy I recommend. Remember, if rent covers your portfolio repayments, what you have is *good* debt. It's worth examining if your desire to reduce debt is due to society's deep-seated belief that *all* debt is *bad*.

2. **Use the domino effect.** Move one of your loans to principal and interest. Start paying off the principal from your excess cash flow. Once you pay the debt on this property, focus your increased cash flow on your remaining total debt.

   Your interest repayments have been reduced because you've already paid off one house. This means you can pay off your next house in an even shorter time.

   This is called the domino effect.

   As each loan or house is paid off, cash flow improves and subsequent loans are paid off faster until you're debt free. This is a reasonable strategy if you're still working. It means you can have a stress-free retirement with solid income. To truly become debt free, or to fast track your wealth building, you may need to use the sell to pay debt exit strategy *and* the domino effect.

My four-year-old the property investor

3. **Live off equity gains.** Neither of the previous two strategies is my preferred. I make interest-only payments and live on increases in equity and rental yield.

   Most people want to own their properties outright. But if a portfolio supports loan repayments and gives you adequate income, why pay them off?

   You could simply have your portfolio at a positive or neutral cash flow position and let it increase in value. Meanwhile, you live on equity gains. If your portfolio value increases faster on average than your yearly expenses, this may be the strategy for you.

4. **Give it away.** If your kids can handle responsibility, you can use this strategy. Simply transfer control of a portfolio held in trust by appointing a new company director. The actual asset never changes hands, so no tax is incurred. You're merely assigning *control* of the asset's holding entity.

5. **Transition to carefree living.** Over the years, we found many people wanted to retire or move to carefree living, but were asset rich and income poor. This is partly why we created ResiFund.

   If it suits their financial plan, investors can sell their assets, clear their debts and pay a bit of capital gains tax. They can then invest in ResiFund, which targets much higher income than a typical investment property.

   Income is realised via regular distributions, plus capital growth when ResiFund property values rise.

As with any exit strategy, the right ownership structure is vital. I'll cover trust structures vs individual ownership later.

Remember, your portfolio will be equity rich and cash flow positive when you exit. An exit strategy is all about minimising tax and maximising returns.

## Dad's tips

- Always begin with the end in mind.
- Exit strategies:
    Sell to pay debt.
    Use the domino effect.
    Live off equity gains.
    Give it away.
    Transition to carefree living.

## Selling: a game of snakes & ladders

Selling an investment property is like a game of snakes and ladders. You climb and climb towards financial freedom, but when you sell it's like landing on a snake. You slide down and have to start all over again.

The best advice is always to hold, hold and hold.

You don't need to sell property to access your profits. Selling kills your profit margin because you must pay capital gains tax (CGT) and agent fees. If you 'flip' properties, you limit your success to a rising market. That's taking a punt, and *smart* investing is about *eliminating* risks, not taking risk on.

---

**'Dad, what's a property flipper?'** A trader who buys and sells property in search of short-term gain.

---

If you want to sell an investment property, consider the advantages and disadvantages first.

## Disadvantages of selling

- Capital gains tax (CGT)

- Opportunity cost

- Legal fees

- Agent sales commissions

- Marketing costs

### Capital gains tax (CGT)

CGT is one of the biggest costs of selling an investment property. You give up to *half* the increased value of your investment to the government. I don't think the government deserves this money, kids. It should stay in your pocket. After all, you're the one who took the initiative to invest!

### Opportunity cost

The biggest cost of all. When you sell a property, you lose the profit from all future market price increases. Ask yourself how much money you'll lose if the property doubles in value over the next decade.

It's always better to buy well and hold for the long term. If you need to access capital gains you should be able to restructure your finance to get to usable equity. This means you avoid CGT and other costs. Most people who sell one investment property end up buying another anyway. Then they have to pay purchase costs again, losing money *twice*.

## Advantages of selling

### Access capital gains

An equity gain exists only on paper until it's accessed by selling or refinancing. I'd rather refinance than sell.

### Reduce debt

The only time I'd seriously consider selling an investment would be to reduce debt to improve cash flow. While this may form part of an exit strategy, I don't advise it if you're still trying to build a portfolio.

## Cut dead wood

You may need to consider selling if you're holding an under-performing property. Some people make the mistake of holding poor investment properties or keeping their home as an investment when they buy a new one. The problem is that most homes don't meet the criteria of a good investment property. It's best to sell your home and buy an investment that'll perform at the required level. Ask your accountant about CGT exemptions available on the primary place of residence; they can be used years after you sell your home.

You may buy and sell several family homes in your lifetime or sell an investment property as part of your exit strategy.

The property review checklist will help you decide a sale price. To choose a sales agent, compare their:

- Sales volume. Is the agent part of a strong sales organisation relative to their competitors?

- Commissions.

- Initial and ongoing marketing costs.

### Dad's tips

- Disadvantages of selling:
  1. capital gains tax (CGT).
  2. opportunity cost.
  3. legal fees.
  4. agent sales commissions.
  5. marketing costs.
- Advantages of selling:
  1. access gains. My choice is refinancing over selling.
  2. reduce debt.
  3. cut dead wood.
- Smart investors hold for growth.

## Cash flow vs capital growth

Some investors use a cash flow strategy and some know that *real* wealth is achieved only with a capital growth property strategy. A cash flow strategy aims to supplement your income and theoretically let you retire at the end. But that doesn't mean you retire *earlier* than with a growth strategy. That depends on your initial available equity and the next market growth cycle's timing.

A cash flow strategy is simple. Identify properties with a rental yield higher than your total expenses, interest repayments and holding costs. Once you reach your desired passive cash flow, you choose whether or not to keep working.

A cash flow strategy has problems. The initial capital required for deposits and costs is now too large for most Australians, making a cash flow strategy near impossible. I'm sure you've realised by now that I'm a capital growth property strategist. Real wealth comes from doubling your asset holdings every 7 to 10 years. You never achieve real wealth by trying to supplement your income.

The properties needed to build a cash flow portfolio are usually regional or on the outskirts of major cities. You're lucky if regional properties double in value every 15 years, so we don't consider them part of a capital growth strategy.

Here's an example of how a growth strategy outperforms a cash flow strategy.

If you invest $400k in a cash flow property portfolio and assume it doubles every 15 years, your initial investment should double twice in value in 30 years (i.e. to $1.6m). While this may seem a lot in *today's* money, it won't buy much in 30 years.

If, on the other hand, you invest $400k in a *growth* property portfolio and assume it doubles every 7 to 10 years, your initial investment should double three to four times in 30 years. If it doubles every 10 years, it'll reach $3.2m. If it doubles every 7 years, it'll hit around $6.4m!

The properties I select using the criteria in this book are cash flow positive a few years following purchase. They then achieve strong long term growth. So I get the best of both worlds.

Be very clear on your desired end position when comparing and considering these two strategies. You can't save your way to wealth with rental income or earned income.

I also want to make it clear that you should never combine these two strategies when building your portfolio. Decide on your preferred strategy and stick with it. If you've already started on a cash flow strategy path and you want to switch to a growth plan, I recommend you sell up and realign your portfolio to your plan.

## Dad's tips

- You can't achieve real wealth by trying to supplement your income.
- Regional properties generally double every 15 years and are not suitable for a capital growth strategy.
- Growth properties historically double every 7 to 10 years.
- Never combine these two strategies when building your portfolio.

## Land vs building

Forget nice houses, kids. Instead, look what's *underneath*. What you're really investing in is land. A house always devalues, but the land is what increases.

That's the golden rule of investing.

**Land appreciates.** It goes up in value. It's an appreciating asset.

**Buildings depreciate.** They decrease in value over time. They're depreciating assets.

Australian tax law says a building has a life of 40 years, after which it theoretically needs to be replaced.

Let that sink in and never forget it. Wealth comes from land. The only purpose of a building is to gather rent to help you cover land holding costs.

Now let's talk about buying property for long-term growth. I'd class a long-term investment as a property that grows in value for 150 years plus. That's because I'm not investing for myself anymore. I'm doing it for you and your kids.

**This is why, for the average person, apartments are bad investments.**

I'm talking wicked witch bad!

Apartments are a flashy investment. There's something cool about the thought of owning one. I should say that I build hundreds of apartments each year. But owning one or two apartments in a tower doesn't meet my long term criteria. Even if apartment prices rose faster than medium density housing (25–80 homes per hectare), I still wouldn't recommend to buy one. Because I know that in 40 years it's going to be a slum. The building will age and sell below market value so a developer like me can profit by knocking it down and building again.

Our fund owns apartments, but we ensure we retain the entire building. That way, we have full control over building management, which lets us maximise the rental income.

When we eventually want to sell, we aim for an institutional buyer to buy the whole building.

This concept of owning a whole building being better than owning a single apartment may seem tricky, so I'll explain the big difference.

As our business grew fast, we moved often. One place we were in was Suite 16 – one of 16 offices in a building where each office had a different owner.

When tenants left, each owner appointed their own property manager and no-one worked together to maximise rent for the whole building. The foyer was aging and broken lifts weren't repaired for weeks. You can see why we left. When we did, Suite 16's owner couldn't get a new tenant. I went past three years later and Suite 16 was still advertised as available.

Imagine being Suite 16's owner and having your income cut by 100%! Had they owned the whole building, their income would've dropped by just 1/16th (6.25%). They could've upgraded the foyer, got things running smoothly, and maybe even renovated to make the building more appealing and maximise their rental income and property value.

Owning one apartment in a big building is the same. You compete with all other owners for tenants and have no control over where money's spent. And, if you lose a tenant, you lose 100% of your income until you can replace them.

That might happen quickly if a building's new, but as it ages and upkeep drops, so does its appeal to tenants. This leads to a drop in desirability for buyers, which leads to a fall in value.

When you control the whole building, you control maintenance, leasing strategy and community management. You essentially control the building's desirability now and well into the future.

If you buy an apartment, think how much land you get with your purchase. Divide the size of the land by the number of apartments. You don't end up owning much land, which is why there's so little potential for long-term appreciation.

That's why I buy medium-density housing that continues to grow in value over the long term. Even if you eventually have to replace the house you still have a sound investment.

---

**'Dad, have I got the golden rule right: land goes up in value and buildings go down?'** Spot on kids; you've got it!

---

People talk about land content ratio (LCR), but don't worry too much about this calculation. If you're buying a house, unit or townhouse on a reasonably sized block for a suburb, it can still be a worthy investment. I strongly advise you to keep clear of small units with low land content, as these are virtually apartments.

Here's a rule of thumb to guide your decisions. The gross floor area of all buildings should, in most cases, be no more than double the land.

In other words, the LCR must exceed 1:2 (i.e. 50%).

Example 1: LCR of a townhouse.
Townhouse = 200 m$^2$
Land = 100 m$^2$
LCR = 1:2 or 50%.
This is fine as an investment; the building is not more than double the land size.

Example 2: LCR of a standard home.
House = 200 m$^2$
Land = 400 m$^2$
LCR = 2:1 or 200%.
This is good; the land is double the building size.

Example 3: LCR of a standard apartment.
Apartment building = 10,000 m$^2$
Land = 1,000 m$^2$
LCR = 1:10 or 10%.
This is bad; the land is only a small fraction of the building size.

My four-year-old the property investor

An old house that needs knocking down may sell with up to 100% of the price comprised of land.

Let's think about supply and demand. When demand exceeds supply, there are more buyers than suitable properties. This pressure on supply raises prices.

When supply exceeds demand, there are more properties than buyers in the market. Prices stagnate or fall until buyers are enticed back into the market.

With apartments, developers can just keep stacking them higher, so it can be harder to get real pressure on supply.

That's why I say steer clear of city centres. As a rule, medium-density housing with good land content always outperforms apartments.

Kids, don't get hung up on these numbers. Just stay away from apartments and you'll be fine.

Never forget the golden rule:

**Land appreciates, buildings depreciate.**

If you like apartments, *rent* one!

## Dad's tips

- Land appreciates, buildings depreciate.
- The total floor area of all buildings needs to be less than the land.
- Wealth comes from land only. The only purpose of a building is to gather rent.
- Don't buy apartments or small units with minimal land content.

## Assets & liabilities: take the good, ditch the bad

The number one reason that 99% of the Australian population are not wealthy, is because they don't understand assets and liabilities.

Kids, let me explain the difference between an asset and a liability.

In the investment world, an asset is something that *makes* you money and a liability is something that *costs* you money.

Look at the list below and decide which is an asset and which is a liability.

1. A good, honest friend who does well at school.

2. An investment property with strong growth potential that puts money in your pocket each month.

3. A schoolmate who smokes, shoplifts or wastes time in class.

4. The family home.

*Answers*

1. Asset.

2. Asset.

3. Serious liability. Don't hang out with that fool!

4. Technically an asset, though it comes with a non-beneficial liability (which I'll explain soon).

We need to distinguish between *appreciating* and *depreciating* assets and *beneficial* and *non-beneficial* liabilities.

You can allow for a liability if it serves a purpose, such as funding an appreciating asset. You need to think hard about non- beneficial liabilities, however, as they'll seriously set you back.

You need to change the way you view everything in life. From this moment I want you to think of everything as either an *appreciating* or *depreciating asset* or a *beneficial* or *non-beneficial liability*.

## The family home

People who consider the family home their greatest asset have no investment strategy. Due to its land content, it is an *appreciating asset*. But it doesn't *make* money; it *costs* you. A home loan is a *non-beneficial liability* because it's unrelated to wealth creation.

## Investment property

An investment property is also an *appreciating asset* due to its land content. A loan for this asset is a *beneficial liability* because it's related to wealth creation.

## Car

Unless it's a rare classic, a car is a *depreciating asset*, since its value reduces over time. Even if you pay cash for it.

Here's my advice on buying cars while building your fortune. Drive the cheapest car your ego can handle.

If your salary is $150k, don't drive a $100k Mercedes; make do with a $20k Mazda.

Don't get me wrong; I own several 'toys' and reckon I've earned the right to them. But I still enjoy driving my old '89 Hilux. Plus it's great for touch parking!

Flash cars do *not* make you a kingpin. With the money you save by being modest, you can hold another property or three.

Kids, some of the worst advice an accountant can give is to buy a *depreciating asset* like a car to reduce taxable income. A smart accountant will advise you to buy an *appreciating asset* like an investment property with good land content.

The table below shows different asset and liability types.

## Assets & liabilities

| Asset | Liability |
|---|---|
| **Appreciating** | **Beneficial** |
| Investment property (land component) | Investment loan |
| Shares (if company is performing) | Study debt (school/university fee) |
| Gold | Business loan |
| Rare artefact (e.g. coin/stamp) | Phone bill (if calls generate income) |
| Bank bill/government bond | |
| **Depreciating** | **Non-beneficial** |
| Investment property (building component) | Hire purchase/car loan |
| Cars | Personal loan |
| Building/fixtures | Credit card (even if not using) |
| Computer | Store credit |
| Furniture | |
| Cash | |

You can apply the asset/liability test to almost anything. For instance, a mobile phone is a *depreciating asset*. Yet depending on whether your calls make money or not, a phone bill is a *beneficial* or *non-beneficial liability*.

# Debt

Now that you understand beneficial and non-beneficial liabilities, I want to talk debt. Society has brainwashed us into thinking we must be debt free because all debt is bad.

This is where many would-be investors come unstuck. You must have confidence in the type of debt you acquire, and an exit strategy. This will reassure you that you're on the right path. When you build a property portfolio, the figures get big pretty fast. If you don't have a system to give you confidence, you may get anxious and lose your way.

My brothers and I sometimes stir your nanna up about the debt we've accrued. Like all mums, she worries about her kids. We reckon it keeps her young if we wind her up now and then. It usually goes something like: 'Hey, Mum; did you hear Bob picked up two more properties and is *another* million dollars in debt?'

Bob knows this is good debt because it's a *beneficial liability*. But our mum is old school and thinks all debt is bad. Yet all her boys have a clear exit strategy and can handle large debt.

My point is, don't be scared of good debt no matter how big it gets. So long as you can service it, and it's part of your investment strategy, you're on the right track.

It's crucial you stay in control of your cash flow. Always keep a cash buffer. Should you lose your job, you need enough to cover loan repayments and other expenses until you get a new job.

**'Dad how do I control cash flow?'** Download a budget template from the internet. The order in which you allocate money is key. Your priorities should be:
1. Debt repayment
2. Rent
3. Food
4. Utilities (e.g. power, water)
5. Savings
6. Clothing
7. Entertainment
8. Toys and holidays

Remember, cash is always king.

## Dad's tips

- Understand the two asset categories: appreciating and depreciating.
- Distinguish between beneficial and non-beneficial liabilities.
- While building your initial portfolio, drive the cheapest car your ego can handle.
- Don't ever be scared of good debt.
- Stay in control of your cash flow. Keep a buffer. Cash is king.

## Property types: the big three

Residential property should form the basis of your portfolio when you start. Historically it has offered the best market growth and rental stability. But it's important to understand other types of property you may want to invest in down the track.

## The big three

Vacant land
Commercial/industrial
Residential

## Vacant land

Buying land that fringes the urban growth boundary (UGB) and rezoning or identifying infill areas for potential subdivision can create instant equity. But it requires far more expertise than you need to build a simple residential portfolio.

---

**'What's the urban growth boundary, Dad?'** It's a limit the government sets to control development growth. It divides urban from regional and high density housing from low.

---

The main disadvantage of buying land is that unless it's farmland, you don't get any rent. This makes it hard to support loan repayments.

Though land subdivision and development is a big part of my life now, it's not a passive investment strategy. It's a profession.

Many people think land development is the way to score big. But they don't appreciate the risks. You need specific industry knowledge to succeed. There's little room for error when conducting a site's due diligence and feasibility study. Getting figures wrong can be fiscally fatal.

Land subdivision and development is a whole other ball game, kids. I'll teach you all about it when you're older.

## Commercial property

Commercial means almost all property that contains business operations, including offices, industrial (factories) and retail.

While I suggest you steer clear of commercial for now, I've built a commercial property portfolio and my company also develops and holds commercial property. With several of these projects underway, we've found commercial and industrial property to be solid assets. As I write, we're constructing a number of multi-level office complexes.

Kids, I'll discuss some advantages and disadvantages of commercial property, but when investing in any property type, it's wise to research state and local council planning websites. Melbourne's Urban Master Plan names six activity centres (Box Hill, Broadmeadows, Dandenong, Footscray, Frankston and Ringwood) in which major revitalisation projects are underway.

New South Wales has urban redevelopment projects in Newcastle, Granville and Redfern-Waterloo.

In Queensland, more than 1000 hectares of prime inner-city land are being redeveloped. Target areas include Eastern Corridor, Fortitude Valley, Kangaroo Point South, Milton, Newstead, Teneriffe, South Brisbane, Taringa-St Lucia, Toombul, Nundah, Toowong, Auchenflower and Yeerongpilly.

Western Australia's Perth projects include Claisebrook Village, East Perth Power Station, New Northbridge, Perth Cultural Centre, Riverside and Perth City Link.

This doesn't mean all these areas hold good investments. I think some would be poor choices. I'm just showing you the kind of information that's out there. If you know the government's planning strategy, you can see the big picture and reduce your risk.

There are three reasons I strongly recommend you avoid commercial property at first.

1. **Tenant stability & vacancy rate**
   A company is only as stable as the industry it's in and the people who run it. Take a hard look at any company wanting to lease your property. You'll need to understand business financials or get an accountant to review them for you. Be very aware when considering a tenant that many new businesses fail soon after start-up.

2. **Valuation assessment**
   Commercial property is mainly valued on its rental yield. It's hard to reduce rent to win new tenants because the property's valuation also drops. There can be long periods between tenants; six months isn't uncommon. Given you rely on rental yields when building an initial portfolio, you may not be able to afford to have your property sitting vacant. Expect a big value decrease when interest rates rise and commercial property demand softens. Be prepared. Keep your gearing low so you have enough cash to service your debt. Expect the banks to come knocking and ask for some of their money back if prices fall.

---

**'Dad, what's gearing?'** It's the loan to property value ratio. Low gearing means there's a lower amount of borrowings against a property.

---

### 3. Finance
Banks know commercial property is a higher-risk investment than residential. That's why they lend only 60%-75% of a property's value. This means you need a much larger deposit.

That said, commercial properties have two main advantages over residential:

### 1. Growth and cash flow
It's easier to find a commercial property which, when tenanted, provides positive cash flow and strong growth potential.

### 2. Tenant make good
The tenant must maintain the property. You provide a shell and they fit it out. When a tenancy ends, they must restore the property to its original condition.

Kids, commercial property investing is riskier than residential, and our initial wealth building strategy is all about minimising risk. Use residential property as your primary form of wealth building. While you may also wish to build a commercial portfolio later, I suggest you wait until you have a healthy level of equity and a strong cash flow. Commercial property cycles (and their underlying factors) differ to residential.

### Dad's tips

- Historically, residential property has offered the best market growth and rental stability.
- Development is not a passive investment strategy.
- Investing in commercial property is riskier. Your initial wealth building strategy is all about minimising risk.
- Stick to your plan.

## Getting started: ready, set, go!

The first deposit is the hardest to save. Once you've started building your portfolio, your appreciating assets help you fund future deposits and you're off and running.

My first house was a tiny, three-bedroom brick veneer on a 900 m² block. (Picture a shoebox splattered with the world's worst colour scheme and an inside paint job that looked like it belonged in a kindergarten.) I still don't know why they called it Bayswater. There was *no* bay and *no* water that I could find!

To get started, I sold my Holden HQ Premier. That was one mean car. I got $3500; big money then. I'd also saved $3000 and there was my deposit. Two Bairnsdale mates moved in with me and helped me pay the interest with cheap rent.

That place needed a lot of love, which became known as the McLellan reno (thanks to your Uncle Al). It cost around $5000. This covered paint, tenant-worthy carpet, classy curtains, a flat pack kitchen, tiling, a bathroom vanity and tan bark for the garden.

Suddenly, along came a little thing called capital gain. That house's value rose by more than 40% seemingly overnight. It was my life's wake-up call. I could never have saved money that fast. I was hooked.

Think outside the square when you're trying to put together your first deposit. Budget and save to prove you can stick to a plan. Ask for help, but know that I'll expect you to show sound investment and exit strategies. OPM isn't easy or free. A cute smile and 'Please, Dad!' won't cut it.

There's nothing wrong with using OPM to get started, provided you know systematic investment basics and show you can stick to a budget and make sacrifices if needed. Think of ways to use OPM to plant your first apple tree. Because by the time you save a deposit, property prices may have jumped again.

I think it's OK to help kids start investing. But it's important not to give them so much that they don't have to do anything themselves.

Another way to start is to buy with someone else. Ideally someone who knows and shares your long-term plan, like a brother or sister. Matt and Al bought their first property together under their dad's guidance, then each went on to create substantial investment portfolios.

Don't buy long-term investments with friends. It may feel safe, but it can get complicated. If one of you ever wants to leverage the available equity to buy a property of your own, this can make things difficult. The situation can also get ugly if one of you wants to sell (not advisable due to the tax you incur).

Kids, I'm in business with friends, but that's very different to holding long-term investments with them. My businesses and development projects give me an income which I then use to buy long-term investments.

## Dad's tips

- Along with your savings, think of ways to use OPM to put your first deposit together. Getting started is the most important thing.
- Avoid long-term investing with friends.

## Sharks

Property investing is a bit like jumping in the sea. It's fun and it feels powerful once you understand compound growth. But under the surface, someone's always lurking, waiting to take a bite out of you, or even eat you whole!

The more you flash money, the more sharks you attract. While they come in all shapes and sizes, they're usually fast talking, well dressed and wearing a tie.

Here's the first rule of engagement. Ask everyone you deal with what they charge and get deliverables upfront in writing. It's not rude, it's just business. If someone won't give a straight answer or put anything on paper, something's fishy. When you smell a shark, swim away fast!

Many people think property agents are sharks. If so, they're not the scary kind. Because you always know an agent's agenda: they want to sell and they'll work *every* angle to make you buy. That's all cool kids, because we're in the property buying game. So long as we understand how agents work and get paid.

There are far more dangerous sharks to watch out for.

### Skimmer

Instead of taking one big bite and making their presence known, these sharks live on lots of nibbles. They charge above market rates for their services and/or deliver less than what was agreed. Skimmer sharks can feed off you for a long time, smiling their toothy shark's smile all the while. This is why it's crucial you always have clear, written agreements. These quickly expose skimmer sharks before they do damage. When they try to put the bite on you, just politely but firmly smack them over the nose with your written agreement. This keeps everyone honest. Don't let people feed off you just because you like them personally.

### Great white

The most dangerous shark of all. The all-powerful great white appears out of nowhere, dazzling you with its fast talk and enormous presence. These sharks eat you whole. In a slow market, they peddle get-rich-quick schemes and 'educate' you on how to buy a granny's backyard and retire on your big score. In a bull market they have a total feeding frenzy. At the first sign of media hype, they smell blood and start hunting for big numbers. You'll see amazing deals like apartments sold off the plan with projected end values based on fast-moving markets.

My four-year-old the property investor

In the early 2000s I was a fairly savvy investor. But I wasn't confident enough to voice my opinion. Before I knew, a close friend of mine was scammed royally. After a free seminar, he was conned into paying $40k to attend a weekend property workshop. During the workshop he was talked into buying two inflated apartments off the plan using $400 deposit bonds. He told me he was going to be a multi-millionaire. Things turned sour when it was time to settle on the apartments. The valuations came in hundreds of thousands under the mark and he was ruined. I still feel sick for not speaking up at the time.

Unfortunately, 3500 Australians collectively lost around $60m in this scam alone.

Some great whites even organise high-interest loans so you can afford their course. How considerate!

I'm not opposed to you paying for education, kids; there's more to learn than what your old man tells you. But if you do pay for it, make sure you know exactly what you're getting and how the new expertise benefits your defined investment strategy.

Signs that sharks are circling:

- Pumping music and high fives to get you hyped. Smart investors don't buy on emotion.

- The presenter tells you about the charity they support. True philanthropists don't self promote. If someone says they're a philanthropist, you can bet they take far more than they give.

- Questions asked multiple times, e.g. Are you ready to change? Are you ready to take action? Are you ready to make the sacrifice? (If you hear these, *you* may be the sacrifice!)

- Act *now*! Reduced price offers during or at the end of seminars.

- No discussion on the risks of investing. This should be the centre of an education session. I always find it amusing that risk is either skimmed over or never discussed.

- The promise of getting rich quick. Remember, smart investors get rich *slowly*.

- Promises of above-average returns.

- Offers of loans to cover more investment seminars.

Know an advisor's motivation. To understand why someone promotes a product or service, you must first understand how they're paid.

Smart investors know a true wealth strategy isn't built on market hype or get-rich-quick schemes. People who try to get rich quick aren't investors, they're speculators. And speculators lose money more often than they make it.

Remember people and process. In life, you're the only person that can make things happen. Invest time in your education and put together a safe investment strategy.

Beware of sharks, kids. I guarantee you'll meet plenty on your journey.

## Dad's tips

- Asking for the cost up front and politely demanding things in writing isn't rude; it's good business.
- Beware of sharks. You'll meet plenty on your journey. Smart investors know true wealth isn't built on market hype or get-rich-quick schemes.
- Invest time in your education.
- Understand and follow a safe investment strategy.

## Fighting the dream crushers

Why do so many people want to invest in real estate, but so few actually do it?

I could write a book on this subject alone. For now, here are some of the reasons people give for not investing:

- They don't have enough knowledge, so they lack confidence in their decisions.

- Fears about repairs and maintenance. They don't want to get up at 3 am to fix a toilet.

- Timing the market. They keep waiting for the market to soften before they buy. The problem is, what if it goes up again?

- Lack of time. People simply don't have time to learn the fundamentals of safe investing. And even if they grasp the basic principles, they don't have time to identify smart investments.

- Money. People don't know how to get the right finance or structure it correctly. They're embarrassed if they're denied a loan the first time they apply. But there are plenty of banks out there.

Another main reason people don't invest is that they listen to others who are too scared to invest themselves. These negative people deploy 'the nasties' – little comments that deflate you. Kids, don't let these comments kill your desire to break free. If you let these motivational vampires stop you from investing, one thing's certain: you'll retire poor. Maybe not unhappy, but definitely poor. When people talk down property investing, they're often trying to justify why *they* never did it. Don't waste your breath trying to change their views. Take no notice, just nod and smile.

Kids, let's look at this another way. If you wanted to bake a perfect chocolate cake, what would you do? You'd mix the right amount of flour with the right amount of water. Then add an egg and maybe some cocoa. Would you take advice from someone who'd never baked? No! You'd probably go and find a funny-hat-wearing, cake-making expert chef with a proven recipe, right? The same applies to investing.

Learn from those with a proven method.

Stay on track. Stick to your plan.

## Dad's tips

- Don't take advice from people who haven't built a property portfolio.
- Block out the nasties. Beware of motivational vampires.
- Stay on track. Stick to your plan.

# Which comes first: home or investment?

Let's talk about your first property.

You can have a home with a white picket fence and a mortgage that feels like jail. Or you can rent anywhere you want and put your money in an investment property.

If you build a portfolio first, you can buy any house you want after a few years.

Your Uncle Bob still rents, even though he has a solid investment property portfolio. Soon after buying his first home, Bob wanted to move. Though in a good area, the house just wasn't where he saw himself with a family down the track. It was no accident Bob's first purchase met all the good investment criteria, so he kept the house in his portfolio. Now Bob is very good with numbers. He worked out that he could rent a much nicer house, in his ideal location and put a tenant in the place he owned. By taking advantage of standard tax benefits, his weekly cash flow also improved.

Matt, my business partner at OpenCorp, has only now purchased his first home. Having built an impressive portfolio of investment properties, he was able to pick the exact home he wanted.

Matt's wife Claire bought a house years before they married. Matt had arranged for her to buy a block of land and build a spec home on it. It was one of eight blocks in a row. By coincidence, I bought one of these blocks too.

Matt flagged the opportunity and Claire sought finance. But the banks messed her around. It was a stressful time. Houses aren't cheap and banks often forget what it's like on the other side of the counter.

Claire told Matt that the bank guy was useless *and* extremely rude. Sadly, this isn't uncommon. Claire didn't want to ever go through it again. She's smart, but this was all new to her.

With persistence, the finance was sorted out and Claire bought the property. Luckily for her, Matt knew how to research. A year later the house was valued at $120k more than Claire paid.

She conceded this was well worth four stressful hours at the bank!

My friend Ady is also building a portfolio and recently bought a property. It wasn't his first, so he should've known the finance broker would lose his payslips and request the same data many times. It was a pain in the backside, but considering the return he'll make, a worthwhile one.

Ady rented while building his portfolio and he loves the security it gives him. He's now safe in the knowledge he has something substantial to pass on to his kids.

Most people want to buy their dream home first because that's the way we're programmed to think. Go to school, get a job, have a family, buy a house. Then spend the rest of your life paying it off. Sorry, but that's just depressing. It's a huge weight on your shoulders. It makes me think of some old movie where the evil guy in a cape cries, 'You shall have a mortgage forrrevvverrr, ha ha ha haaa!'

Sounds crazy, right kids? But that's what almost everyone does.

I quote Einstein again:

'The definition of insanity is doing the same thing over and over again and expecting a different result.'

Kids, we all know rich people do things differently, but most people are too scared to have a crack. They worry it's too hard or that they'll fail. Oh, the shame!

While most people don't love their job, they do nothing about it. So it seems they prefer unhappiness to uncertainty.

Most people can't seem to take the few basic steps to build an investment portfolio and reap the rewards. Instead, they bust their butt at school and university. They work hard, often in complex jobs. Then keep walking the same old path to a very poor retirement. I say *bugger that*!

The thing is, it takes time to learn investing, keep your focus and make the strategy work. That's why I created this guide for you.

New things are stressful. I was so green when I bought my first property. When I went to the agent's office to sign the contract, he asked for my conveyancer's details. I gave him a blank look. 'What's a conveyancer?'

I appreciate the pressure of doing something new with this level of commitment. I have, however, found it's definitely worth the effort. For most people, investing isn't part of their everyday lives. But it's possible to reach a stage where buying property is like picking up new shoes:

You check them out. They fit. And that's it!

## Dad's tips

- Why not rent as you build your portfolio? It's a better financial option.
- Investing can be a natural part of life.

## The 10 biggest mistakes property investors make

- Buy a property close to home (so you can drive past).

- Self-manage tenants (they're a pain; investing should be fun).

- Buy at auction (paying more than everyone else is *not* smart investing).

- Buy an old property (with no potential to add real value).

- Buy based on 'look or feel' (leave emotion at the door; let facts and figures make your purchase decisions).

- Ask a real estate agent for advice (you'll only get answers that favour *them*).

- Overcapitalise (a waste of good equity that could be used for your next deposit).

- Sell to realise a profit (rather than refinance and save tax).

- Pay off debt (instead of creating a redraw facility or using an offset account).

- Fail to have a subject-to-finance clause (this clause, explained later, lets you out of a contract).

- Fail to get an expert to review a contract (unless you can understand the contract to its full extent).

- Buy in regional areas (this reduces growth).

- Not having a risk mitigation strategy (without a system, you only compound risk).

- Wait for a market downturn (what if it goes up instead?).

- Wait for the deal of a lifetime (you may pass up many other good deals while you wait).

- Buy for 'future development upside' on the open market (every developer in the area will have already looked over the deal and decided it's no good before it gets to open market).

- Chase the lowest interest rate (rates aren't the most important thing; I'll explain later).

- Fail to have correct ownership or financial structures in place.

- Fail to allow for all purchase costs (e.g. stamp duty, mortgage registration, lenders mortgage insurance).

- See an approved finance limit as an unconditional commitment from the bank (pre-approval is not unconditional approval).

- Sell property to finance lifestyle (once you're financially independent, create a line of credit and live off the equity gains).

On second thoughts, there are a lot more than 10!

## The main event: property vs shares. Ding! Ding!

Kids, it's crucial to keep control of your investment strategy. To gain financial freedom, you need only buy five investment properties over 12 years. With this strategy, you're in control, so you minimise risk.

But when you buy company shares, someone else has control. They make all the decisions, which means they control your money. You might as well blow it at the casino. I suggest you let your property portfolio create your wealth.

---

**'Why do people argue over property vs shares?'** Because like your good friends the Wiggles, they appear similar at first glance. As both appreciate at around the same rate, it's easy to compare average yearly returns. Dig deeper, you find they're not alike at all.

---

So what makes these two wealth-building investment options so different?

Banks and financial institutions class shares (even blue chip) as a higher risk than property. Once you get to know them, you'll realise banks hate risk. They want to know they'll get their money back. Just look at their loan to value ratios (LVR). Banks lend up to 95% on property, but merely 0–75% on shares. Most banks' margin lending or LVR averages 50% on approved securities. This means they deem shares *twice as risky* as property!

Following the 2008 global financial crisis, shares dropped by around 45%. Residential property, under the median price point in Australian capital cities, dropped by about 10%.

At this time, many people received a devastating margin call from their bank or broker. A margin call means the bank has deemed your shares to be worth less than previously. You're required to deposit additional funds or sell some of your assets.

Because of the lack of control when investing in share and the market's volatility, I'm not comfortable gearing shares at all. Anyone gearing shares at a higher LVR than 50% is much braver than I.

We know wealth is built using OPM. The more OPM you have in a rising market, the more gains you make. Real wealth comes from recognising the value increase in your investment and leveraging more OPM to reinvest. But if you can access only 50% OPM safely on top of your own money (instead of 95%) the long-term compounding effects are staggering.

This graph shows the importance of maximising OPM and the huge long-term differences in wealth if you invest in shares instead of property.

The graph shows a $50k initial investment in each vehicle. Shares get a 50% LVR for a total investment of $100k. Property gets a 90% LVR for a total investment of $450k.

I've factored 8% yearly growth for property investment and even given shares a head start with 10% yearly growth. Look at the difference in growth over 20 years. As you can see, property beats shares hands down. It all comes down to the power of leveraging OPM.

## Property vs shares

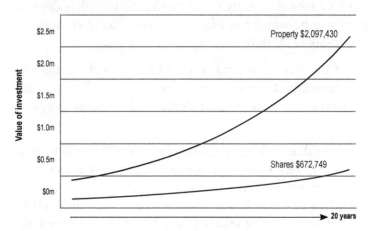

Now kids, remember this is before you even duplicate each portfolio. The graph shows only an initial investment in each vehicle and the compounding effect. If you leveraged each investment's equity, property would further dwarf the returns of shares at 20 years.

Kids, because banks class shares as a higher risk than property, property will always outperform shares as a wealth-growing vehicle.

Most financial advisors recommend shares. That's because they only get paid if you invest in shares (or, historically, in investments they recommend). This doesn't mean their recommendation is a bad investment. It just means it's not the *best*. Most financial advisors are salespeople for managed funds. The industry is changing, with new laws on the disclosure of commissions. If you're getting investment advice, always make sure you understand the advisor's motivations.

I'm pleased to say I now know financial advisors who promote a variety of investment vehicles, including shares and property.

## Dad's tips

- Stay in control of your investments.
- Property will always outperform shares due to accessible OPM.
- Understand an advisor's motivations.

## Buyer activity, price cycles & developer activity

Kids, to understand how to choose quality investments, you need to know how buyers, price cycles and developers impact the market.

Let's look at the different types of buyers and how their purchasing patterns affect market movements and price cycles.

The property market comprises of three purchasing groups by sales volume:

| | |
|---|---|
| First home buyer | 20% |
| Relocator (upgrader or downgrader) | 50% |
| Investor | 30% |

## First home buyer (FHB)

FHBs seek an entry-level home. They want to leave their parents' home or stop renting. FHBs buy at sub-median prices and may want to start a family. They have minimal assets and limited capital. FHBs are highly sensitive to interest rate movements. They're also scared of missing out on the 'great Australian dream'. They buy on emotion, panic when prices rise. FHBs push prices up from the bottom of the market. The price growth cycle is typically started by FHBs as the government provides incentives to them to invigorate a market.

## Relocator/Owner occupier (upgrader or downgrader)

Relocators seek a specific type of property: something bigger, smaller, better, closer to work or in a nicer suburb. They must sell their home for a good price and so need active FHBs in the market to push prices up. Relocators buy on emotion and pay more for a house that meets their needs. Relocators own property at the top end of the market, so when they get active they draw prices up as they buy above the median price point.

## Investor

Investors want to make money. They won't compete on price and, in theory, should never buy at auction. They want to get in before prices boom and their target price will be sub-median (as with FHBs). Investors like to buy at low interest rates. But they're not as 'twitchy' as FHBs as rents often rise at the same time to offset the impact. Investors don't push prices up but they absorb excess stock. This increases the urgency of FHBs to get into the market before they miss out.

Each group has a different motivation; it's important to know what drives their decisions.

Sydney and Melbourne have around twice the sales of Brisbane and Perth. When investors move from a larger market to a smaller one, the demand pressure can invigorate the smaller market as investors soak up excess stock.

Once investors have made money from a growth cycle, they want to take advantage of the increased equity in their properties. If the local market is starting to ease and shift into a slow growth phase, they won't be keen to invest there. So they start looking at other markets where the short-term growth prospects may be more attractive.

## Developer

Kids, when looking at factors affecting supply and demand in different markets, one thing people fail to consider is developer activity. It's vital you understand the massive impact developers have when you're assessing potential markets.

Two main types of developers interest us: medium and high-rise apartment block developers and broadacre land subdividers. Other developers, such as infill townhouses and dual occupancy developers (recreational developers), don't influence the market as much as major developers.

Here are the steps in the development process:

- feasibility and due diligence

- acquisition

- design

- planning approval

- presales

- construction

- settlement (when the resident can move into the dwelling).

Apartment development takes up to three years from concept to end product. Land subdivision and build takes two to three years. I'm talking large apartment blocks (100+ dwellings) and larger land developments (200+ lots).

Look at the OpenCorp developer's activity chain diagram Matt and I developed. The activity it outlines affects the supply of properties, which dictates price movement. This diagram will help you understand why the market *cycles*, rather than growing evenly each year. This is a good concept to grasp, as it shows there's only a very small time window when it's *not* advisable to invest in a particular market.

# OpenCorp developer's activity chain

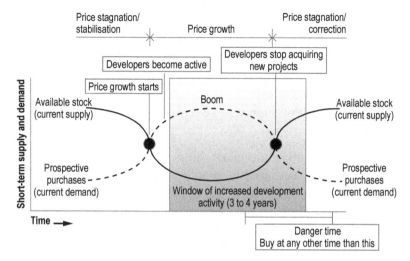

As you study the diagram, focus on the supply and demand lines. You'll see that up to the point where demand exceeds supply, prices have stabilised, corrected or become stagnant.

Investors then start to buy excess stock. When price growth begins, developers see opportunities to make profits again and start buying and delivering stock to the market (this is the shaded part of the diagram).

A large-scale development can take years to bring to market. During this time, a shortage of dwelling stock causes further price growth. This is when a boom often occurs.

Unfortunately, most developers don't get active until they see the boom start. And given it takes two or three years for their projects to deliver new supply to the market, most development stock is ready *after* the boom. This leads to over-supply, as stock can keep coming onto the market for up to 18 months after the boom ends. This is why prices stagnate or correct/fall, then don't pick up again until the excess supply has been soaked up. Typically, when demand drops below supply, large-scale developers stop acquiring new projects.

The market clock example below shows how the real estate market cycle is ongoing. You need to view each city market individually because it moves through each stage at different times. I view the four major cities as eight markets: four residential and four commercial. The clock shows only residential markets. I've indicated the danger time for investors, when you should not invest.

## Market Clock

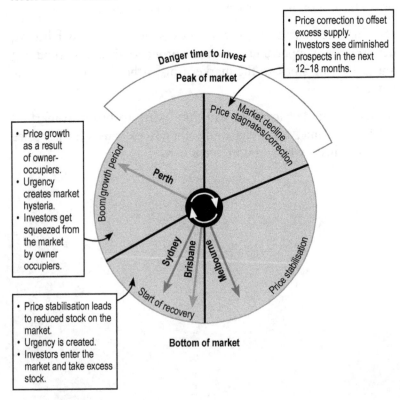

My four-year-old the property investor

As we know, property prices don't rise by 8.7% every year. The market generally follows these cycles over 7 to 10 years when you invest in a growth area. The market may have stagnation and price correction after a period of high growth. But prices recover and boom again. Then you see large price increases over a short time. This is when things get really exciting if you're holding a substantial portfolio.

Once you know how to accurately determine the current position of each market, and which ones aren't worthy of investment at that time, you can choose a market with good growth potential. The faster you achieve growth, the faster you can duplicate. Kids, I'm not giving you a crystal ball. But I am showing you how to understand the market and make informed investment decisions.

---

**'Dad, why don't investors wait and try to pinpoint the right time to buy in a market cycle?'** Considering that prices increase at around 8.7% per year over the long term, it's much more likely that when you buy a property, the market's next move will be up.

---

Remember, there's only a relatively short time in the market's entire cycle when prices may correct and decrease until excess stock is bought. People who wait to buy and try to pick a slight market downturn are playing seriously bad odds.

Don't be put off by the real estate cycle. Booms and dips come and go. Both are expected and neither lasts forever.

You're not a trader; you're an investor with a long-term strategy. That means you buy, hold, buy, hold, buy, hold.

So when's the right time to buy? I once asked this of a wise man. His answer: '20 years ago'. And the *next* best time? 'As soon as you can afford a deposit'. Cheers, Steve; that was the best tip a rookie investor could ever get!

Kids, note the 12 to 18 months after a market has experienced significant growth, when prices stagnate or correct. This is the only time we don't invest. After a market has had years of strong growth, look to other cities. Choosing the right time to buy is actually fairly simple, once you understand this concept.

## Dad's tips

- Understand the different types of buyers and the effect their activity has on the market.
- When is the right time to buy? As soon as you can afford a deposit.
- The danger time for buying into a market is during a late boom, stagnation or price correction period.
- Understand the time it takes developers to bring product to market. After every high growth period, you can expect a market stagnation or correction as supply exceeds demand.

## Sweet emotion

Never get emotional when considering an investment. I collect guitars and I sometimes get emotional and pay too much. Why? Because if I *really* want a particular guitar, I pay whatever I have to. I don't avoid telling your mum what I pay, I just mumble sometimes when she asks.

As you're never going to live in an investment property, you can let go of any emotional connection with it. Conduct your research on the market and area. Stick to your investment criteria and ensure everything measures up. Then buy. Remember there are lots of houses out there to buy or build. If you don't find one that ticks all the boxes right away, move on.

Don't look at an investment property as if you might live in it one day. This is the biggest mistake you can make. Most investors buy within 10 km of their home (i.e. in their own postcode). Why? Because they know and like the area. They go to their *local* real estate agent. But if you rely on your local agent for a property, you ignore 99% of the country's viable investments.

Beware the shark. (I'm hearing *Jaws* music ...)

Don't get me wrong; I know agents who are true assets when it comes to investing. But let's not kid ourselves: agents always play to your emotions because that's the easiest way to sell.

If you look locally, you'll hear comments like:

- It's a lovely safe area.
- Doesn't it feel homely?
- You'll most likely get nice tenants.
- You can drive past the house and keep an eye on it.

Don't fall for *any* of this; it's a complete crock!

If you do your research, you'll know your purchase is a solid investment that meets your strategic criteria. Your mum and I own many houses that we've never seen. I don't recommend this unless you have someone to manage the process for you. My team provides checks and measures that give me control during due diligence. I have confidence in my investment because I have a system to manage risk.

As mentioned earlier, I pay too much if I get emotional. Everyone does. But if you take emotion out of a decision, you can happily walk away. And that means you'll always get the best deal.

My dad told me something when I was young:

'The deal of a lifetime comes up every week.'

Time and again, he's been proved right.

## Dad's tips

- Don't make emotional investment decisions. Industry players will work on your emotions. Be prepared.
- The deal of a lifetime comes up every week, if you know how to find it.

## The money shop

Let's talk banks. Kids, banks are just money shops. You already know that to invest successfully, you must use OPM. The good news is, banks *want* to lend money. They just don't hand it out to anyone. You need to make them feel comfortable about it first. Like us, banks always look to minimise risk when investing their money.

Banks are businesses and under no obligation to lend money to anyone. It's therefore your responsibility (and your finance broker's) to sell you and your property to the bank as a safe, low-risk investment.

So what satisfies a bank's requirements? A bank needs to feel safe about who it's giving money to and what it'll be used for. Each lender has criteria that must be met before it opens the vault.

So why do most people go to a bank with their ideas scribbled on a napkin or, even worse, with no plan at all? This common error shows the bank you haven't planned how you're going to use its money. That makes it very hard for the bank to feel safe about lending to you. Kids, if you take time to understand the bank's lending criteria and build relationships within the bank, borrowing is relatively simple.

Here's what a bank wants to see before approving your finance:

- Proof of income (yours and your partner's).

- Other income sources (e.g. rent or business distributions).

- Rental forecast for the new property. (A local agent can give you an estimate.)

- Your credit history. You can get a copy of your credit file at equifax.com.au. It's not uncommon for an issue to be on file, even if you're not at fault. You can get these cleared up. Try to have a clear credit file before you apply for money. If you have an outstanding issue, explain it so the bank doesn't get a surprise. Once a bank's credit department knocks you back, they take major convincing to change their minds. And each time you apply for finance, it goes on your credit file (so you only want wins).

By understanding these requirements, you can make it as easy as possible for a bank to approve your application.

## What you need from the banks

### High loan to value ratio (LVR)

The less you have as a deposit on a property, the more money you must use on your next purchase. So while you're building your initial portfolio, you want a bank to lend as much as possible on the property's value. I'm talking 90, 95 or even 100%.

You pay lenders mortgage insurance (LMI) on loans over an 80% LVR. Kids, LMI isn't an issue if it gives you usable equity to buy more investments. Ask the bank or your broker how much LMI you'll pay and factor it when buying. After the bank does a credit check, they'll go to one of a couple of insurers for LMI approval.

---

**'Dad, what's mortgage insurance?'** Mortgage or loan insurance, also known as lenders mortgage insurance (LMI), is a policy a bank takes out to protect itself on any loan over an 80% LVR.

---

## Debt to service ratio (DSR)

The banks want to know you can make repayments and still have money to live. Each bank has a slightly different way of determining DSR, but generally they want to see that you earn around 1.5 times the interest. Most banks take 80% of rental income into account when assessing your DSR. The actual calculation is your income, including 80% of rental income, divided by all your expenses.

## Valuation

It's important to understand the valuation process. A fair market valuation from a real estate agent assesses what a property would sell for on the open market in a reasonable time (usually 60–90 days). For a bank panel valuation or lenders mortgage valuation the instruction is much different. What the bank request is the figure that the property will sell for on Monday 9am. Obviously there will be a big difference between the two figures. 5–10% difference is expected. Anything more is sign that something is wrong. When you deal with a bank's consumer area, you may not be able to control the valuation process, but I strongly suggest you try.

Compile data on sales comparable to the investment you plan to buy and give it to the bank when you apply. Try to get the valuer's details. Make sure they have your sales data and know the valuation figure you wish to achieve.

It's far easier to give comparable sales data *before* a valuation than to move them up from a poor one. It's up to your bank or broker to go into bat for you if a poor valuation comes in.

Valuers get paid regardless of what price they put on your property. And they always go low unless you provide comparable sales data. Some valuers and banks do in-house 'desktop' valuations (meaning they don't leave their desk to carry it out). They simply use median house prices, other limited data and analytical programs. This is another reason you need to show the valuer comparable sales. The easier you make their job, the better.

If a bank needs to call in a loan on a property owner who fails to meet repayments (a mortgagee sale) the valuers may be financially liable if they're found negligent in their assessment of the property's value. They, or their insurance company, pay the difference unless they can show similar sales or other evidence to support their valuation.

Here's an example of how vital it is to control the valuation process. Say you need a deposit of 10% to buy an investment property. If you have five investment properties, each valued at $400k for a total of $2m, you need just a 2% increase in value across your portfolio to buy *another* $400k property. Because that 2% increase gives you another $40k (10%) deposit! But if you fail to control the valuation process, you don't get the additional amount required for deposit, meaning you can't duplicate.

Valex is making it much harder to ensure a reasonable valuation, because it limits prior communication with valuers.

---

**'Dad, what's Valex?'** It's not a valuation firm as it doesn't do valuations. It just distributes valuations to a panel of qualified valuation firms on a lender's behalf.

---

## Loan structure & security

As you build your first portfolio, I advise you not to cross-secure your loans. While banks will try to push you into it, I suggest you use multiple lenders or find a lender that lets you have each loan secured against a single property. Because as your properties increase in value, you'll want to arrange a line of credit on each one for future deposits.

---

**'Cross-securing loans, Dad; what does that mean?'** It means more than one of your properties is used as security for a single loan.

---

So why don't we want to cross-secure loans?

Look at the diagram below. Property 1 has equity available that can be used as a deposit on Property 2. If you approach Bank ABC (where you have your current loan) they'll try to cross-secure each property and use the equity on the first to buy the second. This locks both properties together.

## Cross-secured structure

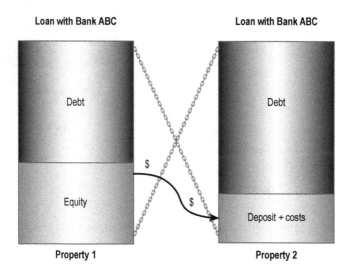

There's a downside to this.

If, for some reason, you can't meet Property 2's repayments, the bank can sell Property 2 *and* Property 1. This can also give you less flexibility to duplicate later.

Now look at the next diagram to see the advantages of using separate banks while building your portfolio. Each loan stands on its own. By creating a line of credit against Property 1, you can use this as the deposit for Property 2. This set-up has two main advantages.

# Line of credit structure

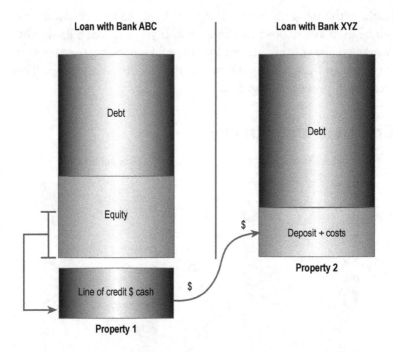

First, it means neither bank can sell your whole portfolio (though unlikely, this isn't a risk worth taking). Second, it gives much more flexibility when it's time to duplicate.

Say you have three properties in different states, and one market goes up. If the same lender finances all three properties, the two properties that haven't moved dilute your equity.

But if your properties are with separate banks, you needn't have them all revalued. You just revalue the property that's gone up and access the additional funds. This process is far more complex when properties are secured against each other.

Kids, once you've built a portfolio of 10 properties or more, this becomes less of an issue. When you have several properties in a couple of states, you may wish to group them with one bank and establish a single line of credit.

Similarly, you should never cross-secure your home with your investments. Trust me; the bank will keep trying to sign your home as security. There's no reason for them to do this, so tell them loud and clear the answer is NO. Use the equity in your home for investment deposits by having a line of credit in place.

## Charges & guarantees

Educate yourself about the impact of fixed and floating charges on your companies or trusts and get a good grasp of directors' guarantees, especially if a bank has intent to secure your home into the loan equation. Have your solicitor review all contracts until you understand them. Quiz your solicitor on the impact of conditions in a loan contract.

---

**'Dad, what's a fixed and floating charge?'** It means a bank can appoint someone to sell the assets of a company (or person) if they default on debt payment requirements. The charge 'floats' until a default occurs. If the bank exercises the option, the charge then crystallises and becomes fixed and the defaulter can no longer deal or trade those assets.

---

**'So what's a directors' guarantee?'** It means the directors of a company have personally guaranteed a loan, making them personally liable. Banks prefer fixed or floating charges because smart directors never own anything.

---

## Interest rates: fixed or variable?

Banks stack fixed rates in their favour, so I use variable, interest-only loans for my investments. I pay only the interest component of the loan. As I have an exit strategy, I'm comfortable not reducing the principal with standard repayments.

Always compare rates between banks. It's OK to pay a slightly higher rate if a bank gives you the right structure (e.g. a higher LVR) and doesn't require crossed securities. You can always refinance or renegotiate later (unless, of course, you fix your rate). If you can get 95% LVR from a bank with a higher rate than a bank that'll only approve 80% LVR, I suggest you take the higher rate, so long as you can cover repayments. Because this means you have more available equity for your next deposit.

## Determining your borrowing capacity (BC)

Your BC comes down to three key factors, your:

1. Debt serviceability ratio (DSR).

2. Deposit.

3. LVR.

Your DSR is your income divided by your expenses. Income includes 80% of market rental income from investment properties, your earned income and any other income you receive.

The deposit you must contribute depends on the LVR you achieve.

Lenders may have slightly different criteria when determining your BC. Find a good broker (the best way is via referral) and be very clear on your BC before you seek a good investment.

You'll need to do a basic budget (the internet is full of templates). Use your budget for at least six months so you know how much you can dedicate to loan repayments. If you can save an allocated amount each month without fail and you're happy with your lifestyle, you're ready to buy.

## Bank internal overview

A bank's attitude towards you changes as your portfolio grows and your business becomes more valuable. It also depends on local and global economics.

The next diagram outlines a bank's internal structure. You'll operate in the retail/consumer space for your first dozen properties. There you can get up to 95% LVR with the help of mortgage insurers. Each bank area has different lending rules. Many people make the mistake of dealing only in the commercial area for their business trading and personal wealth creation. It's important to separate business banking from personal wealth creation banking. While commercial banking may lend only 60–75% of an asset's value, the private wealth creation area will lend 80% or higher if negotiated.

If you clearly present your proposal to a bank each time you apply, the staff start to see your investment strategy. This helps them align you with the right bank area. And when that happens, the bank becomes a valued partner in your wealth creation.

## Bank overview

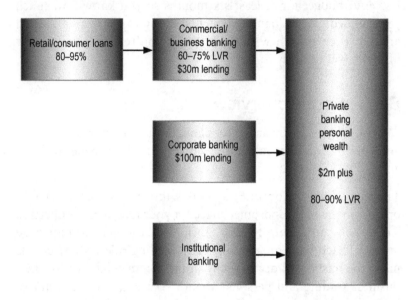

## Credit cards

Though I have credit cards for my businesses, I don't have a personal credit card. I use a *debit* card for personal purchases. A personal credit card can reduce your DSR considerably. Why? Because banks deem you to have the power to max it out! They then deem you to be paying the maximum monthly repayment and factor this into your DSR. This can hit you hard when you're trying to get a loan pre-approved.

Kids, if you have a credit card, get rid of it. It's pure evil. Imagine if the bank were red and 10 feet tall, with horns and a pointed tail. Well, the credit card is the pitchfork in its hand.

A credit card is a short-term, high-interest loan designed to take the most money from your pocket in the least time possible. Yet credit cards are cleverly marketed so it seems logical to use them in daily life.

Banks pay brokers fees to get clients on credit cards. So always specify that you don't want a credit card under any circumstances. Cutting up a card isn't enough; you must cancel the account. Use a MasterCard or Visa debit card for personal needs.

If you have enough for a deposit plus costs, it's time to go shopping. If you need more money, start saving or find some OPM. When buying investments, you must first determine your BC. Then you'll know exactly how much you need to get started.

## Dad's tips

- A high loan to value ratio (LVR) gives more usable equity for future deposits.
- Make sure you understand the bank's debt to service ratio (DSR).
- Control the valuation.
- Don't cross-secure properties when building your portfolio.
- Don't cross-secure your own home.
- Understand charges and guarantees.
- Be clear on your borrowing capacity.
- Cancel credit cards.

## School smart vs street smart

School taught me nothing about money. This never made sense to me. I figured that since our culture thought money was evil it shouldn't be discussed.

As a kid, I asked my dad how much he earned. All I got was a clip over the ear for my troubles. My parents were small business owners, but they still had issues discussing money. They owned a newsagency and a motel before they took bad advice from someone they trusted and lost the lot. Seeing them in business, though it didn't end well, gave me confidence to try my own ventures. Their experience also flagged potential pitfalls and why it's vital to eliminate risk with a systematic approach.

One day, my teacher said he'd teach us about investing. I sat up very straight in class that day. He gave us a copy of the newspaper and we each had to pretend we had $10k to spend on shares. We followed the share market for the next few months to see if we'd made money.

I actually chose some pretty good shares. My only error was to tell the teacher I thought it was the dumbest investment strategy ever. To me, it was no different to gambling.

The project did open my eyes a bit, though. I started noticing the cars my teachers drove and realised they had no idea about finances either! Sorry teachers, I mean no disrespect. Two of my sisters-in-law teach and both are building property portfolios. They're smart teachers. School was no place to learn about wealth creation; I had to find another way.

Once I realised how easy it was to invest in property, I made it a mission to talk to every investor I could find. I wanted answers. I was hungry for knowledge and itching to put everything I'd learned into practice.

Kids, I'll level with you: I wasn't school smart. But you can't compare school smart to street smart and say one is better. I wish I could turn back time and absorb all that knowledge. I used to laugh at teachers going on about maths, accounting and law and wonder why I'd ever need to know these things. How silly I was! I now use those very skills daily in my business and investing life. Come to think of it, taking a few more notes in English would've helped me write this book and Matt wouldn't have had to do so many corrections. (Thanks again Matt!)

School smarts strengthen and complement street smarts.

Today I can easily keep up with accountants and lawyers. But it cost me a lot of time and money. For years, your Uncle Al and I drove our lawyers and accountants crazy. We asked the same questions over and over until we both understood the explanation. A painful process, but worth it. We now have a crack team of accountants working for us full time. Your mum jokes that our accountants know more about our lives than we do!

What's the message here? You won't learn about money in school, but if you study hard and learn school smarts, it makes your street smarts a hell of a lot sharper later on.

Stay in school kids. Study hard and I'll teach you about the investment world.

## Dad's tips

- School smarts complement street smarts and make them stronger.
- Don't mock what you're taught at school.
- Study hard. Knowledge is the foundation to successful investing.

## Mirror, mirror on the wall, who's the richest of them all?

Property investors, of course!

Kids, you need to understand something about money: it's not as scarce as many people say.

Every year, more money flows into our country. The chart below shows real money in circulation (currency) as well as monetary promises.

## Australian monetary circulation

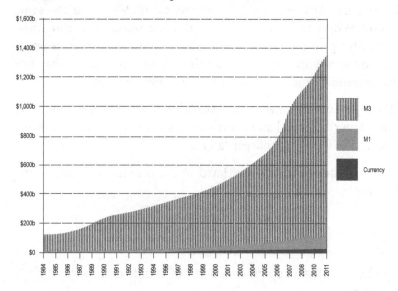

My four-year-old the property investor

This ABS information shows that the amount of money in our economy has increased significantly. In the last four years alone, the flow increased by $400b. This is partly due to China buying Australian minerals. If this continues, the next 20 years will see a massive influx of money into Australia. We're currently the world's second-largest iron ore exporter. This will only increase with China and India's demand. In addition, our liquefied natural gas (LNG) projects will soon start generating revenue.

Australia has around 8.9% of the world's coal reserves and 1.6% of its natural gas reserves. We export 30% of the world's iron ore. When you consider that we have just 0.3% of the world's population, we're set to become one of the world's wealthiest countries per capita.

Sadly, despite all the extra money circulating, most people still believe it's hard to come by. This is because money flows through our economy like a stream and collects in pools. People who work for a living sit beside the stream with cupped hands, trying to catch enough to feed their families.

Investors know money flows downstream. Instead of trying to catch it, they dig channels (investments) and divert the stream into their own pools. If you try to do this with earned income or slow-growth investments, such as property that has a cash-flow positive focus rather than growth, you'll only ever grab enough to survive.

But if you acquire smart investments (growth properties), money will always flow abundantly in your direction, especially if you dig your channels in the right places with the right investment tools.

I'll now explain the various income types and how each relates to the money flow.

## Earned income

Earned income is income you generate through work (i.e. salary or wages). This includes any moneymaking activity that requires your time. So if you have a job, work as a consultant or own a business that needs your input, you generate earned income.

When you work to earn an income, you're trying to catch money in your hands as it flows downstream.

## Trading income

Trading income comes from selling something for more than you paid. Trading is like digging a hole in the sand. It fills up when it rains but quickly drains away when things dry up.

Trading income includes:

- Shares or paper assets.

- Real estate trading (remember, flipping isn't investing).

- Buying and selling goods for profit (e.g. cars, antiques, collectables).

Trading income is riskier than other types. You must correctly predict a market to keep buying and selling at the right time. I like studying markets but I'm no fortune teller. Trying to predict short-term market moves, especially with shares, is a tough gig. Remember our motto, kids: eliminate risk, never take on risk.

## Passive income

My favourite income derives from assets you create or buy.

The two main passive income areas are:

- Property that produces a positive cash flow and equity growth.
- A business that requires little input from you.

True passive income continues to flow year after year with very little effort on your behalf. With passive income, your pool of money keeps growing over the long term, and you don't have to keep dipping your hand in the money stream.

The easiest passive income to set up and manage comes from a residential property portfolio. Smart investors focus on channelling this type of income stream.

### Dad's tips

- Channel money into your own pool and make it work for you by acquiring investments that provide passive cash flow and equity growth.
- Understand the different types of income.

## Stick to your plan

It's easy to get off track when you invest in property because, in reality, it's just so easy. Once you buy a property and get a tenant, there isn't much more to do except sit back and wait for value growth. It's actually pretty boring.

In my early days in business, the money I made in a whole year was nowhere near what I made from my portfolio growth. And while the time spent managing my portfolio was minimal, I had to work hard on my business all year. Once set up, a portfolio is easy to manage. You can 'set and forget' until your next portfolio review. Too easy!

Kids, there's one more thing you need to know about the flow of money. As money flows along the channels you've created, they get deeper and wider. The longer you invest, the faster you accumulate wealth. At this point you need to reinvest quickly, buying multiple properties at a time while still controlling risk. But let's face it, kids; there are worse problems to have.

## Temptation

I know people who built substantial wealth but lost it. Why? Because they changed strategy or kept investing everything they had to chase the next big score. In other words, they kept stacking straw. I advise you to build your portfolio with lots of little bricks. You needn't buy a 10-storey tower just because you can. Why not buy several residential properties instead? It's safer to invest in lots of small, solid investments than a few big ones. While building your initial portfolio, remember this old saying: 'small fish are sweet'.

Once you've created your investment plan, don't deviate from it in any way. Before long, you'll start accruing serious equity and this will bring temptation. Over the years I've looked at many different investments, including share and trading strategies. I've reviewed business ideas, acquisition opportunities and endless variations on property investment.

While many of these were tempting, I invested in very few, mainly because I didn't know them as well as my own strategies. If I'm not educated about an investment, I steer clear until I know the risk and return.

Kids, money can cause jealousy. Whatever you do, don't get the 'jealousy jitters' and feel you must act on an idea or miss out.

Close friends have told me I should invest in a pre-public share offering for a company they'd checked out because the information memorandum looked good. It's easy to feel you're going to miss out by not acting on these offers. But stick to your guns. You know your strategic plan works and you're going to have more wealth in the long run. So why deviate?

Wait until you've built substantial net wealth and plenty of spare cash before you try other investment strategies. Many wealthy people live by this theory. Put your eggs in one basket and watch that basket very carefully. In other words, stick to what you know. Never bet the farm.

Kids, always remember the important things in life. Once you've achieved a comfortable level of net wealth, the rest is just a bunch of zeros on a page.

## Dad's tips

- Lots of small, smart property investments are safer than a few big ones.
- Let opportunities pass if they're not part of your plan.
- Build substantial net wealth before trying other investment strategies. Don't bet the farm.
- Never be jealous of the success of others. Whoever dies with the most toys does *not* win!

## Contracts: think first, don't just 'sign here'

Get everything in writing. I repeat – get *everything* in *writing*. In business, I've formed the habit of asking people to email me everything from meeting minutes to verbal agreements. It keeps me organised. More importantly, when you have everything in writing, there are no grey areas.

I write my own contracts where possible. If you use someone else's contract to do a deal, the terms will always favour them.

Never sign anything unless you understand every part of it. Contracts are like 'choose your own adventure' books. If a clause cites a section, go to that section and read it. It might say, 'you skip through a daisy garden and everything is fine'. Or it could say, 'you've just been eaten by a dinosaur'. Take time to check contracts in full and make sure you understand each clause before you sign.

Don't be fazed by legal jargon. Legal concepts are, for the most part, logical. It's just that lawyers have devised certain words and phrases that aren't in everyday use, so they seem complicated at first. But if you pay attention and keep asking questions, you'll quickly learn.

When you start, you may feel you're asking all the stupid questions. But that's good. People who ask lots of questions end up with all the answers.

Kids, you won't believe what people will try on. Agents I've done business with for years have tried to slip terms into contracts that weren't part of our verbal deal. From ridiculous exclusive sale agreements to uplifts in fees. Rest assured they never made that mistake twice. Read *every* contract, even if it looks like every other contract you've seen.

Avoid property deals where projections factor price rises or future market lifts. You see these deals everywhere in a strong market, and not just on apartments. And in case you didn't listen to your old man earlier, I'll say it again: don't buy apartments!

If you're not 100% confident with a contract, have someone experienced explain the detail. Then sign knowing you're making the right decision.

## Dad's tips

- Get all agreements in writing.
- Learn to love navigating your way around contracts.
- Don't sign unless you understand everything in a contract.
- Consult your legal team before signing.

## Prenuptial agreements

Kids, get used to the idea of a prenuptial agreement.

It's a tough conversation, but one that must happen. Fortunately, your mum and I met when neither of us had a cent, so we didn't need one.

I won't talk about love, except to say I wish your world was all chocolate rivers and gum drops. But sadly that's not the case.

You must have a prenuptial agreement before you move in with someone. Even if you own just one investment property. Don't risk all your hard work because you're too uncomfortable to have the conversation with your partner.

Kids, you know I'd rather be the fun guy. But a prenup removes all doubt so it's a good thing. I don't necessarily agree with a 'your money/my money' scenario. But I believe initial assets should be protected.

If your partner won't agree to a prenup, be concerned. If they lay a guilt trip on you, or say they're offended, don't fall for it. Give them time to digest the idea, but remember: if they're *not* in it for the money, they'll happily sign.

Some of my staff built serious portfolios and had to have the chat with their partners. All got prenups and all couples are still together.

Current laws stipulate that if someone stays in your house for three months and proves you had a relationship, they have a right to *half* of *everything* you own. Don't risk losing the farm just because you came down with a case of puppy love.

Ask your partner, if the tables were turned, would *they* risk everything they'd worked for? If they say yes, they're playing games. There's no need to risk your investments for a relationship. Smart investors eliminate risk. Someone who cares for you will never impose risk on you.

I wish you only happiness, but don't get soft. Your lawyer will be able to draw up a standard prenup. Consider it a part of life.

## Dad's tips

- A relationship should never mean you have to risk your investments.
- You must have a prenuptial agreement in place.
- Be prepared to discuss a prenup with your partner. Open and honest communication is key to a lasting relationship.

## Structure: to trust or not to trust?

There are several types of trust. For a property portfolio, a standard discretionary family trust is suitable.

**'Dad, what's a trust?'** It's an arrangement where property is held 'in trust' (by a trustee) for the benefit of others (the beneficiaries).

There are two ways to hold property: in your own name or in a trust (which means the property is held 'in trust' and you control the trust).

**'Dad but why use a trust?'** It may sound complicated, but this form of control has advantages. Also, trusts aren't as complex as they seem once you understand the terms and laws that apply to them.

To understand trusts, we must travel back in time to look at where and *why* trusts came about.

As far as I can tell, trusts were first used around 400 BC when the Greek philosopher Plato set up a not-for-profit trust to fund his university. The first trusts to hold property were set up in England in the 11th century. By the 15th century they were common.

Trusts were mainly used by landowners to protect their land from greedy lords and kings. Back when knights rode horses and swung swords, there were hundreds of taxes and limitations on what people could and couldn't do with their land. If a king or lord found a landowner had committed a 'crime', they could throw him in jail (or worse) then seize his land and leave his family with nothing.

This was why smart landowners moved the ownership of their land to trusts, which meant they weren't bound by the same tax rules and limitations as individuals. More importantly, their land was protected. If they were found guilty of a crime or sent to war, the king or lord couldn't take the land because the trust owned the land, not the individual. Instead, the landowner's family could assume control of the trust and the land. The land never changed hands, so there was no tax when it was transferred to the family or heir.

## Should you use a trust?

Today we still have tax laws like in the old days. We also have a very real need to protect our assets.

Laws determine how trusts operate. And who makes our laws? Politicians. And how do politicians and rich people hold assets? Believe it or not, most use trusts. While there are no guarantees, there's a good chance any law changes will favour trusts. The diagram below shows the people and entities involved. I'll describe each role.

# Trust overview

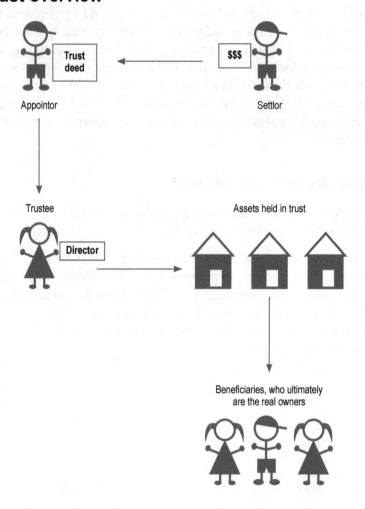

Appointor

$$$

Settlor

Trust deed

Trustee

Director

Assets held in trust

Beneficiaries, who ultimately are the real owners

My four-year-old the property investor

# Beneficiaries

These are the people a trust is designed to benefit.

Kids, if all profit made by a trust went to one person, they could pay the highest tax rate. But because trust income is spread among beneficiaries, each person pays tax at their marginal rate. Spreading the income achieves the lowest overall tax rate.

The trust may pay tax on behalf of beneficiaries but retain after-tax funds for reinvestment and safekeeping.

The tax advantage of a trust may not seem huge. But as years pass, profits flow. Why give money to the government when you can keep it in the family?

There are a few types of beneficiary, but it's usually someone related by blood or marriage. You can make a company a beneficiary and you or your family will own that company. If you distribute enough profit to beneficiaries, you can put extra profit into a beneficiary ('dumping' or 'bucket') company to be used later. Why? Because companies pay just 30% tax. When beneficiary incomes exceed *their* tax bracket, they pay a higher rate.

## Trustee

A trustee can be one or more people or a company. A trustee manages the daily operations of the trust. I have several trust structures and use companies as my corporate trustees. As director of these companies, I maintain control.

## Settlor

To set up a trust, a settlor must give a small amount of money, to be held in trust. I normally use my accountant as settlor. I never use a family member, as a settlor can't benefit from a trust.

## The Appointor

The appointor is the most important person in a trust. I sometimes refer to them as head honcho, big dog, kingpin, drill sergeant, big cheese, boss or chief. The appointor has the power to appoint or sack a trustee.

Kids, it's very important for *you* to be the appointor.

When getting a trust set up, ensure you're the appointor. If the person setting up the trust is unethical, they may name themselves as appointor. This means they can sack you as trustee and take control of your property. You'd instantly lose everything held in that trust. This is a very scary scenario, so always check your documents.

# Advantages of trusts

1. **Control**
   You own nothing but control everything.

2. **Asset protection**
   This is the most important thing a trust can offer. There are plenty of scumbags out there who'd start a lawsuit for a few easy bucks. Sadly, Australia is becoming more like the US in this regard. If someone tries to sue you, your first move is to sack yourself or the company (because you're the appointor) as trustee. With this done, there's no link for anyone to access the assets. And thus no reason to sue.

3. **Income distribution**
   You can distribute income across your family and pay a lower tax rate.

# Disadvantages of trusts

1. **Loss of negative gearing**
   Negative gearing means you can offset losses and reduce your taxable income. This is seen as an advantage when you own a property in your name. With trusts, you don't get this immediate tax benefit. You can, however, carry these losses forward and offset them against future profits. Initially you may buy the first few properties in your name until you've built enough equity to cover holding costs.

   The small initial tax advantage of holding a property in your name is far outweighed by the distribution and transfer of control benefits of holding property in a trust structure. You and your family will be better off in the long run by using trusts.

2. **Fees**
   Accounting fees are higher when everything is held in trust. Take into account that the set-up fees and yearly accounting fees will also be higher, because the tax return is slightly more complex.

### 3. Borrowing

Finance is more complicated and you need a broker or relationship manager at the bank who understands trust lending. Most do these days.

Make sure you get your structure right. The right structure for you will be determined by your income type, business owner or employee. It may also be determined by the size of the portfolio you want to build and your exit strategy.

Kids, the right structure is essential. Get it right from the start.

## Legal will

Get your lawyer to prepare a legal will. Every financial plan needs an exit strategy because sadly, we all take a final bow. This is very important. If you have no legal will, your assets may be distributed against your wishes and this can get very messy. You built your portfolio, so make it clear who benefits from all your hard work.

---

**'Dad, what's a will?'** It's a simple document with clear instructions on how assets are distributed once you kick the bucket.

---

### Dad's tips

- Understand the roles associated with trusts and their function.
- Advantages of trusts:
  - control
  - protection
  - income distribution.
- Disadvantages of trusts:
  - tax losses are carried forward if held in a standard trust
  - set up and accounting fees.

## Tax: pay, but don't tip

Every Australian is morally and legally bound to pay tax. It's important you pay the right amount and not more. That's why when you invest you need to set up the right financial structures with an experienced accountant.

Kids, here are some of the services the government provides with our tax. Whether it's spent wisely is debatable.

1. Infrastructure projects
   Roads, bridges, tollways and other projects.

2. Public security
   Police, fire departments and defence forces.

3. Health services
   Free or subsidised health services like immunisation shots and Medicare.

4. General services
   Road cleaning, water treatment, streetlights, rubbish removal and, of course, the building and maintenance of public parks and playgrounds.

5. Education, government wages, maintenance of historic monuments, unemployment benefits, government aid, retirees, emergency relief, social housing, government departments like department of agriculture, commerce, energy, urban development, treasury, judiciary, department of this, that and the other.

All this and more is funded through taxes.

## Types of tax

Governments impose taxes in many forms. These include income tax, goods and services tax (GST), carbon tax, council rates, payroll tax, Medicare tax, capital gains tax (CGT), stamp duty and land tax. With petrol, the government even taxes a tax by charging GST on fuel excise!

How does the tax system work?

Australia has a marginal tax system common around the world. The more you earn, the higher your tax rate.

The downside is that it doesn't encourage people to work harder, which would strengthen our country.

In our tax system, a person on a higher income pays a higher tax percentage than someone on a lower income. I think it should be the other way round. Low and average income earners often expect rich people to pay more tax. Why?

Imagine I'm a gardener.

Picture me with all the other gardeners, shovel in hand and ready to dig.

We each get paid $1 for each tree we plant.

In the first year, the guy next to me plants 50,000 trees. I work twice as hard to plant 100,000.

Why should I pay a higher tax rate than someone lazier than I?

Now let's say I get entrepreneurial and buy a planting machine. It costs me a lot of my heavily taxed income to buy this piece of machinery. I'm taking a big risk. But the risk pays off and the next year I plant even more trees.

So why should I pay a higher tax rate than someone who not only doesn't work as hard as I but also doesn't take the risks I take?

I can't see things changing dramatically, but we're a lot better off than most countries. That's because Australians always question and look to improve the system.

The good thing about our tax system is that it does offer some benefits to investors. While the government may not pay us to work harder, it does encourage us to work *smarter*.

Here's how.

Taxable income = gross income less business-related expenses.

This is why rich people often pay less tax than their employees who earn less. You have to pay income and capital gains tax only on the money left after expenses.

So with property, the best way to minimise tax and improve the compound growth of your wealth is to hold onto it.

It's important you make tax work for you, by learning the terms.

Before-tax dollars = gross income.

After-tax dollars = net income.

When you earn income, you pay tax and live on what's left. When you invest, you earn income, pay business-related expenses and pay tax on what's left.

This diagram shows the huge difference in income flow for employees vs property investors/business owners.

## Income flow

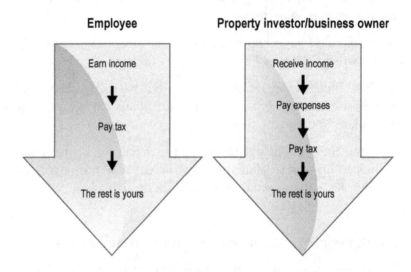

## Depreciation

Each year investments (the buildings) depreciate. This can be deducted from taxable income. Yet around half of property investors don't claim depreciation! Seriously; I couldn't believe it either. Get a depreciation schedule and ensure you claim every cent.

---

**'Dad, what's a depreciation schedule?'** It's a report that shows the depreciation allowances an investor's entitled to. There are two types of allowance available: depreciation on plant and equipment, and depreciation on building.

---

My four-year-old the property investor

Plant and equipment means items *in* the building (e.g. oven, dishwasher, carpet, blinds). Building allowance refers to construction costs *of* the building (e.g. concrete and brickwork). Both these costs can be offset against your assessable income.

Depreciation is the best tax benefit you'll find. Apart from paying to have a depreciation schedule drawn up, you needn't spend money to claim it. If you buy a property built after 17 July 1985, the tax office says that property will depreciate over 40 years (after which, in theory, it's worth nothing). Remember, buildings depreciate and land appreciates. The rule lets us offset against income at 2.5% of construction cost. Fixtures, fittings and furniture depreciate faster.

Get a quantity surveyor to do a building depreciation schedule for your accountant so you can maximise the offset allowed. Even the schedule's cost is tax deductible.

I've often had to remind accountants doing my tax to include depreciation. Check your return in detail and never assume your accountant has covered everything.

Which expenses can you claim on your investment property?

Here's a standard list of deductions:

Accounting and tax agent fees
Advertising
Agent fees or commissions
Bank fees and charges
Cleaning and gardening costs
Council and water rates
Depreciation of building
Depreciation of furniture and fittings
Depreciation schedule
Electricity and bills
Home office
Insurances
Interests and other borrowing expenses
Land tax
Legal fees
Office supplies
Pest control

Postage and stationery
Repairs
Security
Telephone
Tools if used solely to repair the property
Travel.

Keep your receipts (i.e. tax invoices) so your accountant can work out what you can and can't claim. Keep them in a concertina file under the above headings so you'll be ready at tax time. Every receipt you fail to keep is an expense you could've claimed. Keep them *all*.

## Negative gearing

Negative gearing is when income from an investment property fails to meet the expenses of holding it. The amount you're out of pocket can reduce your taxable income.

If you invest in a trust (as I strongly suggest you do) the out-of-pocket amount will reduce the taxable future profits of that trust. If your trust doesn't have another income source, you won't have anything to offset your tax loss against. The deferral structure is probably the only major downside to trusts.

Kids, there's so much hype about negative gearing you can often see the fins circling. Some property sharks will actually try to sell you property on the basis that you'll *lose* money.

Read that last sentence again. It's a sad fact that many people buy on negative gearing alone. Reducing taxable income is great when you're building an investment portfolio, but it shouldn't be your *prime* motivation.

**'But Dad, isn't negative gearing a *good* thing?'** Kids, reducing taxable income is very handy when building a portfolio, but never make the mistake of thinking it's good to spend $1.00 to make $0.50.

Think about our long-term investment strategy: positive cash flow properties with strong growth potential.

This table shows how two people on the same income (a property investor and a non property investor) fare over 10 years. I've used the actual figures of a client who earns $120k a year and bought a house for $412k. See how the end holding costs are relatively low given the equity growth over time.

## Investment vs no investment

|  | Income | Yearly tax paid | Tax refund due to property holding | Holding costs per year | Equity at year 10 |
|---|---|---|---|---|---|
| Non-property owner | $120,000 | $34,450 | $0 | $0 | $0 |
| Property owner | $120,000 | $23,114 | $11,336 | $4,108 | $438,057 |

If you're a pay-as-you-go (PAYG) worker, you or your accountant calculates your tax refund at the end of the financial year. As the Australian Taxation Office (ATO) (Mr ATO to you, kids) knows most people are terrible at saving, the taxman makes employers withhold and remit tax from employee pays.

Instead of waiting until the end of the year for a refund, you can pay less tax from your earned income at each pay period during the year. Get your accountant to review your situation and explain how this works. Lodging a Withholding Tax Variation form (see ato.gov.au) lets you do this. It works the same way as claiming costs on a work vehicle.

You'll need to tell your accountant you have legitimate business expenses related to your portfolio. These include all or part of your car, phone and home office expenses, local travel and, if you have property interstate, travel expenses and accommodation. Seminars, books, newspapers and any education relating to your business activities can be claimed. Keep a clear understanding of what's acceptable, as tax laws change.

Some people are tempted to bend tax laws. Don't do it, kids; always pay what you owe. Life's too short to carry guilt and you need to sleep at night.

Pay the taxman, but don't tip him.

As we've discussed, one of the great benefits of property investment is that tenants and the ATO pay most of the holding costs. If you invest in a trust, you may not get these tax deductions back until your trust is positive in net income.

This chart shows approximate proportional holding costs for a standard investment property. As you can see, you, the investor, pay the smallest proportion of these costs.

## Proportional holding costs

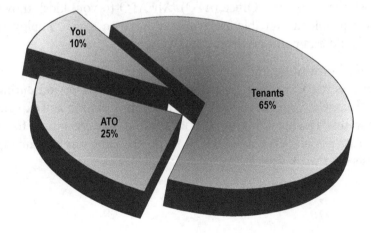

My four-year-old the property investor

- Beware of CGT. Our tax system encourages us to hold property, not sell it.
- Understand the flow of income.
- Keep all your receipts and claim every legitimate expense.
- Don't break the law.

## Superannuation: do it yourself

Superannuation (super) is the government's mandatory savings plan for Australians. It was far cheaper for the government to tell business owners to pay a percentage of each employee's wage into a super fund than to budget and fund people's retirement with old-age pensions.

One socioeconomic issue facing Australia is an ageing population. According to the ABS, baby boomers account for nearly 40% of the workforce and 21% of current retirees. This will put huge pressure on our health and aged care systems.

---

**'What's a baby boomer, Dad?'** A member of the relatively large generation born between 1946 and 1964.

---

It's also predicted that our economy will slow as our current workforce exits. To counter this, the government is trying to increase population with immigration. Though our birth rate is increasing, we need more people in the workforce to keep the economy functioning.

We're better off than many countries on the baby boomer front. Along with income support and super, the government is encouraging potential retirees to stay in the workforce for longer.

A few years ago, I was so disillusioned with institutional super funds that your mum and I went set up our own SMSF. I was sick of hidden fees and poor investment returns. I had no control or clarity on how the fund manager was going to improve my superannuation nest egg, so I went and found out how to DIY.

Every investment option has risk but I felt our super would be much better managed under my control.

---

**'Dad, what's a SMSF?'** It means self-managed superannuation fund. Imagine your SMSF as a bank account that you control. If you don't have a SMSF, that bank account is controlled by one of the institutional funds. They make investment decisions on your behalf. A SMSF means you take control of that bank account and invest in assets you choose.

---

The stock market will crash around three times during the average person's retirement. Property also moves in cycles, but handing money to a diversified fund manager to invest gives me little confidence. Especially when bank lending criteria show they believe shares to be *twice* as risky as property!

When I've met with share-centric fund managers, I've remembered the saying:

'Why would someone who travels by Rolls-Royce ask someone who takes the train to invest their money?'

I'm not a fan of Rolls-Royces, but you get the point!

The chance of a fund achieving premium returns across a diversified portfolio is slim. If one investment does outperform, it's often weighed down by the rest that don't.

---

**'Dad, what's a diversified managed fund?'** One that invests in various assets to 'spread' the risk.

---

**'Diversification is for people who don't know what they're doing.'** Warren Buffet – arguably the world's greatest investor.

---

There are legal obligations and audits your accountant must perform when you manage your own super. When you've mastered property investing, think about managing your super. With your new investment expertise, you'll know your super is much safer when you control it.

## Dad's tips

- Look to manage your own super fund once you're an educated investor.
- Understand diversified funds, their risk mitigation strategy and potential returns.

**Part three**

# The good stuff

# The straight line to wealth

This chapter is really important, kids. It's time to sit up and take notice of your dear old Dad.

As you know, I like to keep things simple. It's my secret to running multiple companies and property portfolios while staying fairly relaxed. I have no trouble switching off when I leave the office (most of the time anyway). If you want to stay married, this is very important.

How do I do it?

I've built rock-solid systems for my investments and businesses and I have tools and reports to keep track of them.

When I started property investing, I didn't have a clear strategy; it was like driving a car blindfolded. I wanted to eliminate risk and take control. That's why I created the straight line to wealth and the circle of duplication.

The straight line to wealth guides you in choosing an investment. The circle of duplication gives you a system to manage your portfolio.

I first used a straight line method when I was in sales. I later adapted it to the straight line to wealth.

I started in sales at 17, negotiating with fruit and vegetable traders at Melbourne's Footscray markets. I learned a lot from those tough, in-your-face negotiations. Later, I worked as a telemarketer, and used everything I'd learned at the markets to sell Telstra products over the phone. I worked in Telstra's call centre for close to two years. And in the last nine months, I was the number one salesperson out of over 120 salespeople every month. Not by a small margin either.

I'm telling you this as I need you to know how powerful the straight line method can be. And also because every dad wants their kids to think they're the best, (give me a break here)!

One day at Telstra, I was called to the managers' monthly meeting. For a kid in his early 20s, it was scary standing before all the big bosses.

They wanted to know how I consistently outsold everyone else. I explained that I visualised a straight line from the start of each call to the end. They looked at me blankly. There was a long pause; so quiet that I expected tumbleweeds to roll past, like in an old Western movie.

I told them I imagined a straight line with points along it. If I went off track, I knew which point I was up to, and so could easily redirect the conversation. I explained that I'd once heard the fastest way to a given point was a straight line – and that's what I visually created as part of the sales process. They stared at me like I was talking in code. But it seemed logical to me.

So, kids, think about how we drive to the shops. Why do we go the same way every time? Because it's the most direct. We know it gets us where we want in the shortest time. We're also familiar with this route, which means it's the safest.

In the early 2000s, when I started training sales teams, I showed them my straight line method. I trained hundreds of staff with this diagram and wrote scripts for each point on the line. I also built objection-handling techniques around them. My straight line method became the key to our business' success.

Your Uncle Al used to laugh at my straight line. He reckoned I must have been on a spiritual journey when I dreamt it up. What he actually said was, 'Are you on drugs?'

But Al knew the power of my seemingly crazy ways. He's one of the best sales people you'll ever meet. He worked with me at Telstra and later we sold on the road for our own business. We enjoyed the constant pursuit of sales perfection.

The straight line to wealth

In 2010, Al and I went to see Jordan Belfort, aka the Wolf of Wall Street (who was convicted of crimes related to stock market manipulation). Jordan and I had something in common (and no, it wasn't jail time!) I ran ethical businesses. Jordan talked about why he was so far ahead of the sales curve. How he'd even had a top neurologist analyse his thought process during a sale! His method has proven so successful that US financial and banking institutions now use it. He described it as 'the straight line method of sales' and he drew this on the board.

●━━━━━━━━━━━━━━━━━━━━━━━━━━━━━━━━━━━━━━━●

Al turned to me and said two words: 'Fxxx off'. Yes, that's right kids; your Uncle Al has a potty mouth.

I wasn't shocked that someone else had worked out this method. To me, the straight line is too logical a concept. And it's definitely the key to delivering sales results.

Kids, selling is fun; I suggest you try it. Most effective business people are also effective influencers (another way to describe a salesperson). I'm glad to say the sleazy, fast-talking salesperson is close to extinction. When you do see one of these dinosaurs, they stand out like ... well, they just stand out.

Modern sales have evolved far beyond this; today's decisions rest on value solutions and support. Solving emotional pain is the easiest sell. And the ability to sell is one of the most valuable business skills. Selling teaches you how to control a situation. It lets you question people's motivations and identify their pain points. In this way, you understand their needs and can predict their next move.

Yet you don't need sales skills to be a smart investor. When I started investing, I wanted a system to give me confidence and control over each step of the process. It's no fluke I build successful property portfolios, sales teams and businesses. I can do it because I plan the required process and oversee each step.

It's like how pop stars can have hit after hit. Their management team follows a formula for song writing and marketing to give them the best chance of success. They follow a business plan.

I list the straight line to wealth steps below and discuss some of the problems you may encounter. Part 4 of this book links to tools that'll keep you on track.

With no system, investing can be overwhelming. That's why many people don't get past the idea stage.

But *you* now have an overview of investing, which should give you the confidence to start.

Mark my words, kids; this is one of the most powerful tools you'll ever see:

**Dear old Dad's straight line to wealth.**

# The straight line to wealth

- **The idea**

- **Setting up your team**

- **Finance pre-approval**

- **Identifying the investment**

- **Contracts**
  Securing the investment
  Established or land and building

- **Finance**

- **Settlement**

- **Construction** (if required)

- **Tenant**

The tools and checks will help you to complete each section

# Tools & checks for the straight line to wealth

**The idea**

**Setting up your team**
Team members details sheet

**Finance pre-approval**
Pre-approval form

**Identifying the investment**
Market review form
Area review form
Investment property identification form

**Contracts**
If building, complete builders due diligence checklist
Have your legal team check all contracts prior to signing

**Finance**
Finance checksheet

**Settlement**
Conduct a property inspection
Alert your property manager and provide keys
If building, alert builder and confirm start dates

**Construction**
Engage an independent building inspector to
monitor construction quality

**Tenant**
Have your property manager complete a prospective
tenant checklist

It really is that simple. When you visualise each step and have a system to eliminate risk, investing isn't so scary. You tackle the first step, finish it, then move to the next.

Each step may bring some headaches. But with the straight line you can take each problem on the chin and keep pressing ahead.

Sometimes, despite doing all the checks you can, you may still feel uneasy. This is when you need to dive in head first. Your mum has a strong character, but she doesn't like this part much. But I love it. Commit to the leap and enjoy the ride.

Back yourself.

The straight line to wealth's power is the strategic process and the checks built into each step – all designed to minimise risk.

## The idea

OK, kids; you're schooled up and ready to start investing. As you know, I value education and research. But now it's time to act.

To be an investor, you need to buy property.

## Setting up your team

To set up a team, you need to make calls and talk to people. Who do you need on your team?

1. Accountant

2. Conveyancer or solicitor

3. Broker or bank

You don't need all-stars. As you have the knowledge and motivation, you can't rely on others. Your team members need only be competent in their field.

## Find a good accountant

Like doctors, accountants specialise in different areas. Just as you wouldn't let a foot doctor operate on your eyes, you need to hire the right accountant. Interview several until you find a fit.

Do not expect accountants to provide you with financial advice. It's not their job to offer financial advice or wealth creation ideas. While they can advise you on the tax implications of wealth creation ideas you show them, many aren't licensed (or financially secure themselves) to tell you how to invest.

So, kids when talking to accountants (and financial planner alike) ensure that they are not advising you on what's out of their scope of expertise. Similarly, many financial advisers don't get paid to recommend property as an investment. Many are not permitted to do so based on their licensing requirements. So, understand they may not be able to recommend all available investment options.

A financial adviser's primary objective is to not loss a client's money. This is not a bad thing, but it does mean that many are not effective at building wealth.

---

**Diversity is for people who don't know how to invest**
– Warren Buffet

---

Accountants *can* advise you on the structure you need to protect assets. They'll put the right amounts in the right columns and tell you if you've made or lost money. That's their thing. Some of my most valued advisers are accountants and the job they do is crucial. It's taken years to find the right people for my team. The accountants I work with today are far more conversant with property than most. Your accountant will be a great asset when you find the right one.

When you talk to an accountant, ask for their hourly rate and a quote for doing your tax return. Ensure they quote everything upfront and in writing. It's OK to pay more for an accountant specialising in property portfolios. Most accountants will say they're familiar with property investing. Ask for specific information, like how many houses they and their clients own. Watch their eyes: if they glaze over, or start talking big picture waffle, it's a sign they're unsure of themselves.

Find an accountant with property investment expertise and ask questions. Learn all you can about accounting and tax law.

## Conveyancer/solicitor

Your conveyancer or solicitor makes a deal happen. They check all is in order and do the settlement for you. You give them the vendor's statement and sale (or building) contract before you sign. If you're unfamiliar with contracts, get your solicitor to check everything for you. They coordinate everything with the broker, banks and vendor.

---

**'Dad, what's a vendor's statement?'** This document must be given to you *before* a contract of sale is signed. It should give specific information about the property in question. In Victoria, this document is called a Section 32 (from the Sale of Land Act).

---

My four-year-old the property investor

The tasks your conveyancer performs are straightforward. Work with them to understand the process. Here's what they should do for you.

## Purchaser process

- Purchaser gets advice about contract of sale and vendor statement
- Contract of sale signed
- Cooling-off period (where applicable) expires
- Conveyancing practitioner advises purchaser on insurance and measurements
- Vendor's statement prepared and signed by vendor
- Caveat lodged
- Title search and relevant certificate applied for
- Mortgagee requirements attended to
- Requisitions received and answered
- Deposit release statement received and sent to purchaser with advice
- Transfer of land prepared and sent to purchaser for execution
- Notice of acquisition prepared
- Transfer of land sent to vendor
- Statement of adjustments and settlement statement prepared and sent to vendor
- Statements and account details sent to purchaser
- Settlement arrangements made
- Final inspection done by purchaser
- Final search of title
- Where necessary, balance of funds obtained from purchaser
- Settlement attended
- Purchaser advised of settlement
- If there's no mortgage, transfer documents are stamped and registered
- Relevant authorities notified of ownership change

Ask for a quote that includes searches for the purchase and settlement of a property.

# Broker

I recommend using a broker while you're finding your feet. They help you deal with banks and should ensure you get the best-structured loan. I used brokers in the early days and held my head in my hands many times as a result. Brokers tend to overpromise even when they're clearly out of their depth. I could tell you stories that'd turn your hair white. The truth is, anyone with a car and a suit can be a broker. Good brokers are rare. Ask someone you know for a referral, use them until you no longer need their help. As your portfolio and financial knowledge grow, you'll establish direct relationships with the banks.

What matters is that they can get the deal done, with the right structure, in the time required.

Like agents, brokers are salespeople, so look out for fins. You need to know if they're out of their depth. Test them by asking for information by a deadline. If they can't do that, they'll struggle when the heat's on.

Banks pay brokers commissions, so you needn't pay them. As brokers essentially 'sell' loans to banks, they usually push the bank that's offering *them* the best deal at the time.

A broker can be an asset when you're building a portfolio. A good one will get you the right loan. It's OK to pay a bit more to get the right deal structure. For example you might pay a slightly higher interest rate, extra fees or LMI if you can get your LVR over 80%.

Ensure you know why a broker recommends a certain bank. It's not always in *your* best interests. The bank with the lowest interest rate will often have the strictest criteria. They can afford to offer the lowest rate because they incur fewer defaults. This makes them hard to deal with and very inflexible. In my experience, when a client has issues with a bank leading up to settlement, or over a builder's progress claim, it's usually because a rogue broker has recommended the cheapest (i.e. lowest interest rate) loan.

Remember the important factors when building a portfolio:

1. Never cross-secure properties. Use available equity from each property for future deposits and to cover interest repayments during construction.

2. Use less of your own money to begin with. A high LVR loan will let you duplicate faster because you have more usable equity for your next deposit.

3. Use the team details sheet to assemble your team.

# Team details sheet

## Accountant

| | | | | |
|---|---|---|---|---|
| Company name | | Accountant name | | |
| Address | | Number of staff | | |
| Office number | | Mobile | | |
| Email | | | | |
| Hourly rate | | Tax return fees | | |

| Tax planning? | Y | N | Tax returns? | Y | N | Setup trusts? | Y | N | SMSF specialists? | Y | N |
|---|---|---|---|---|---|---|---|---|---|---|---|
| Prepare withholding variations? | Y | N | Trust compliance? | Y | N | Trust setup fees | | | | | |
| Will the principal handle the account? | Y | N | If 'no' who will, and what is their experience? | | | | | | | | |

## Conveyancer

| | | | | |
|---|---|---|---|---|
| Company name | | Conveyancer name | | |
| Address | | Number of staff | | |
| Office number | | Mobile | | |
| Email | | | | |
| Conveyancing rate: sale $ | | Conveyancing rate: purchase $ | | |

| Can they prepare contracts? | Y | N | How many settlements per year? | |
|---|---|---|---|---|
| What searches do they recommend? | | | | |
| What is the cost of the searches? | | | | |

## Broker

| | | | |
|---|---|---|---|
| Company name | | Contact name | |
| Address | | Number of staff | |
| Office number | | Mobile | |
| Email | | | |
| What lenders do they work with? | | | |
| Do they capitalise interest? | | | |
| How much involvement with prepare/review of documents? | | | |
| Do they have a checklist to help me prepare my application? | | | |
| Do they provide and disclose valuation? | | | |
| Do they have the ability to contest a bank valuation? | | | |

My four-year-old the property investor

| Lenders | | | |
|---|---|---|---|
| Bank name | | Contact name | |
| Address | | Position | |
| Office number | | Mobile | |
| Email | | | |
| Line/setup fees | | Interest rates | |
| Types of loans available | | Discounts for larger amounts | |
| Who will I deal with after loan setup? | | | |
| If I pay my builders deposit with cash, will the bank reimburse me at settlement/adjust funds provided at settlement? | | | |
| Does the bank sign off on own mortgage insurance? | | | |
| Do they only accept valuations via Valex? | | | |

The straight line to wealth

## Pre-approval

Once you've assembled your team, you need to determine your borrowing capacity (BC). The following pre-approval form will help you document everything. Follow the website link in Part 4 for full-scale versions of this and all other tools.

If you don't get approval right away, it may not be the amount or structure you wanted. Don't be fazed. Ask the bank what they need to approve you. An inadequate broker or banker can undermine your application. So if you're not happy, go elsewhere. If a bank says no, regroup and try again.

Safely file copies of all documents you give to all parties. I mean everything. Pay slips, contracts, tax returns, the lot. So many times I've been asked for the same documents more than once. By the same *and* different people.

Here's some of the documents you'll need for pre-approval.

1. Your most recent payment summary (the old group certificate) and three recent pay slips for PAYG applicants, or business financials for the last two years and ATO notices of assessment if you're self-employed.

2. Existing loan statement on any debt facility (e.g. home loan, personal loan, credit card (if you're silly enough to have one).

3. Rental statements or lease agreements for current investment properties.

4. A rates notice for each property you own.

5. Driver's licence and/or birth certificate.

Remember to check equifax.com.au to ensure you have a clean credit history.

Once you get pre-approval, have your broker specify the amount in writing.

Make sure you know how much you can borrow, how much you need to contribute and, more importantly, when you must come up with the funds. It's vital you determine your BC before your property search. Otherwise you're wasting your time. Be clear on who's providing the funds for stamp duty, loan setup fees, mortgage insurance and legal costs. Are these costs included in the loan or will you pay them from your own pocket? If you're considering a land-and-build package, do you pay interest on drawdowns at each construction stage, or is interest capitalised on (i.e. included in) the loan?

---

**'Dad, what's a drawdown?'** Also called a progress draw, it's a payment to the builder at each building construction stage.

---

Find out how long it'll take to get unconditional approval from the lender so you can add this clause to your contract. The clause should read: *the sale is conditional on finance approval from 'specifically named' bank*. If you don't specify and name your preferred lender on the contract, you may be forced to find a second or third-tier financier, and that's far from ideal.

Before you apply for pre-approval, ask for a list of basic terms for the loan contract (including rates, term, fixed and floating charges, guarantees and penalties). These terms must be agreed before your application goes to the bank's credit department. If you're unhappy with the contract, ask for the terms to be changed or removed, or find a different lender.

Once you know your BC, it's time to find an investment.

# Pre-approval form

| Document | Check-off Application 1 | Check-off Application 2 |
|---|---|---|
| Last year's group certificate and two recent payslips (for PAYG application)<br>**OR**<br>Last 2 years' business financials and ATO notices of assessment (self-employed applicants) and personal tax returns. | | |
| Existing loan statement on any debt facility (home loan, personal loan, credit card, etc.) | | |
| Rates notice for every property owned | | |
| Driver's licence and/or birth certificate | | |
| Have obtained a copy of credit report (equifax.com.au) | | |
| Medicare card | | |
| If no property owned, bank statement showing savings history | | |

| Pre-approval details | | | |
|---|---|---|---|
| Lender | | | |
| Contact | | Contact number | |
| Email | | | |
| Rate | | Set up fees | |
| Charges | | | |
| Guarantees | | | |

| | Amount | Date required | Provided by |
|---|---|---|---|
| Deposit | | | |
| Pre-approval amount | | | |
| Legal costs | | | |
| LMI | | | |
| Titles registration | | | |
| Interest payments during construction | | | |
| Stamps and fees | | | |

## Identifying the investment

When you seek an investment, it's tempting to look at actual properties first. This is a trap for rookies. If you do it, you'll quickly be overwhelmed with options. It's a bit like trying to find your favourite lolly in a mixed bag by closing your eyes and dipping your hand. If you want to maximise your opportunities, you must first sift out all the options you *don't* want. You'll find your favourite lolly faster if you tip the bag on the table and discard those you don't like.

Here are criteria for choosing quality investments. This is how it's done.

## Investment target

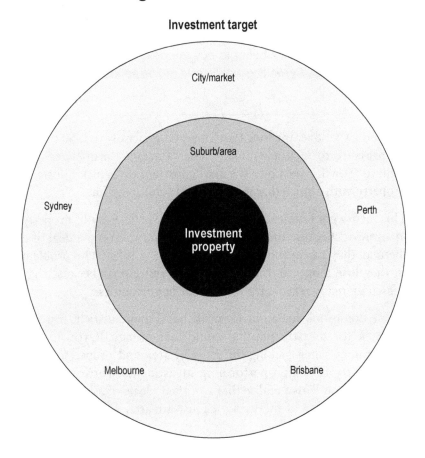

**Investment target**

- First, choose a city market with the best growth potential.

- Second, find an area with a balance of yield, growth and good infrastructure.

- Third, pick the optimum size and quality investment property for the area.

What I say next may seem odd, but bear with me. Instead of seeking a suitable market and area, it's much easier to knock out undesirable markets first. This means you're left with the best investment options.

---

**'Dad, what if I use the MAP process, identify the perfect investment, but can't afford to buy that property?'** Great question, kids. There's an old saying in property: all boats float on a rising tide. The MAP process will give you the best investment at any point in time. But if you can't afford that property, use the criteria to find one you can. It's better to buy the next best thing than to sit out of the market. By waiting, you'll miss out on serious money when prices rise.

---

We know that over the long term, markets generally rise. So there's no pressure to pick a winner. Chances are our properties will achieve growth over time. What we must *not* do is pick a loser; a property with a price that may stagnate for a long time.

This theory goes against what many people believe about property investment. Because they think they may stumble on the deal of a lifetime, they can spend their lifetime waiting for it. The problem is, they lose money in the long run and retire poor because they passed up many reasonable investment opportunities.

So we don't look for an investment that'll make us rich. Instead, we look for investments that could lose money. If you follow this strategy when picking the market, area and property, you'll consistently find high-performing investments worthy of your portfolio. You'll also realise that so-called 'deals of a lifetime' can be found any day of the week; it's just a matter of knowing how and where to look.

## Choosing the right market for you

Now, remembering our strategy of first looking where not to invest, let's see which markets we should avoid. When investing for growth, we consider only cities with more than a million people. I buy in Melbourne, Sydney, Brisbane and Perth because they have more than enough solid investments to meet my needs. I don't invest in smaller cities because the government's population growth predictions are less favourable than for the major cities. The other reason is that I don't understand the fundamentals of all the other markets; and if I don't know what drives a market, I don't invest there.

## Risk avoidance

1. Growth trends

    Avoid markets that have experienced strong growth over the past two to three years. Go back to the developer's activity chain in Part 2. When housing has been in short supply, high growth occurs, leading to high development activity. By the time this stock comes to market, the need has passed. The result is a price correction and a flat market that can last for 12 to 18 months. During this time, it's wise to find another market to invest in. Avoid markets that have experienced more than 15% growth for two years running (e.g. Perth in 2008 after booming through 2006 and 2007).

2. Look for population growth and low unemployment statistics. When I compare capital cities, I don't look for the biggest population growth in recent years, I look for *ongoing* growth greater than 1.2%.

Again, I don't look for the lowest unemployment rate. I just note if one is higher than other cities. For example, look at the performance of Perth and Brisbane after the 2008 GFC. While both cities were booming before the crash, both suffered significant job losses due to the resources slow-down. This meant those cities had significantly higher unemployment than Melbourne and Sydney – both of which performed well over the following three years.

Prices were flat in Perth and Brisbane during this time, but now they look poised to resume a positive growth cycle as the uncertainty over employment dissipates. Remember, kids; when people feel insecure about their jobs, owner-occupiers don't buy new houses. And as you know, owner-occupiers drive price growth.

These four cities are good markets to invest in long-term. But you must reject city markets that aren't at an ideal stage in the pricing cycle and look to markets better positioned for growth. The market review form will help you.

# Market review form

| | Last two years median price growth % (API Magazine, abs.gov.au) | Constant population growth over 2% per annum (abs.gov.au) | Unemployment rate (abs.gov.au) | Stages of the market • boom • stagnant • unhealthy • speculative | Viable market Y/N |
|---|---|---|---|---|---|
| Melbourne | | | | | |
| Sydney | | | | | |
| Brisbane | | | | | |
| Perth | | | | | |

**Area or suburb:** Find the right area to invest in and avoid risk.

1. Employment. Look for areas with employment generators (defined below) nearby. Forget areas with few employment opportunities within commuting distance.

   Also consider the area's proximity to:

   - the CBD (though remember not to invest in or around a CBD due to continual supply)

   - industrial areas

   - activity centres, specifically major activity centres with commercial office accommodation and diversified employment.

Don't be fooled by employment generators like regional mining. Investing in these areas can be highly profitable but it comes with huge risk. Consider Gladstone, a northern QLD mining town that's saw significant growth due to mining contracts. For a few years there was huge employment growth, due mainly to infrastructure demands. While this happened, industry thrived and housing boomed as developers pushed to build enough homes to meet demand. Now that the infrastructure is in place, jobs have dwindled and prices and rents have plummeted. Once the infrastructure is complete, only 30% of the jobs in Gladstone will remain for the duration of the mining contract. This will leave a significant housing oversupply when everyone leaves town.

Mackay in QLD was the most recent 'road kill' in the post-mining-boom come down. As commodity prices fell, mining companies cut spending to soften the revenue dive. I spoke to the managing director of a conveyor belt engineering company. He said, 'Cam, it didn't slow down; it dropped off a cliff in pretty much a week!'

Imagine what would happen to prices in one of our major cities if 70% of the population vacated.

Mining towns have historically been boom and bust. It seems apparent that this trend will continue. Therefore, when considering my family's long-term investment plan, mining town investment isn't entertained.

2. Watch out for a potential oversupply of new dwellings.

   Are there large tracts of land with development potential between this area and the CBD? Draw a line on a map connecting the area you're looking at to the CBD using the most direct route. The line should not cross water. Are there any large areas of undeveloped land along this route that could be brought to market?

   The reason we look for land tracts separating your investment area from the CBD is that we don't want the investment to stagnate due to new supply coming onto the market that offers a cost-competitive alternative for owner-occupiers. Kids, people will happily move towards the CBD if they get the chance and this will reduce demand in the area where you want to invest. Large land developers want to profit as fast as possible so they can reinvest in new developments and report a healthy internal rate of return (IRR). In their project feasibility, they'll have factored multiple stages and they'll bring those to market at competitive prices to move stock as quickly as possible. If necessary, they'll undercut the market to achieve their sales target. Only in later stages will prices rise if the developer wants to capitalise on dwindling stock.

   Developments of thousands of lots can take up to 20 years to sell. Some suburban fringe areas have as many as 15,000 lots ready for development. While these suburbs may be great to live in, I certainly won't invest in areas like this until all cost competitive alternatives in better locations are gone.

3. Ensure the majority of the homes in the area are owner occupied. Also check volume of units in the area. Unit occupancy figures can distort owner occupier percentages but will have little influence on tenant demand for houses. Target areas houses that are within a 4 week timeframe to lease.

4. Access to essential services. Check that the area has:

  - Schools, including primary, secondary and private.

  - Convenient retail, including local shops and major centres.

  - Public transport.

  - Parks and sporting facilities.

5. Check if there's a planned future quality of housing for the area (i.e. a minimum level of housing quality that can be built). You can find this by checking the building design guidelines with the local council or developer.

If you can't tick these boxes, look elsewhere.

**Area:** Value indicators.

Check if there are plans for the area that may add value to your investment. For example, investment in new infrastructure like roads, shopping centres, private schools, rail or employment generators that'll attract more people. Once you've gone through this process a few times, you'll have a good understanding of each city. By now you'll have knocked out large sections of the city market you want to invest in. Once you've identified a worthy investment area, it's time to find the right property in it.

# Area review form

| Area for consideration | | | |
|---|---|---|---|
| Employment generators (proximity to CBD, industrial, activity centres) | | | |
| Oversupply of housing between area and CBD (draw straight line) | Y | N | |
| Majority of homes owner occupier, excluding units (RP Data) | Y | N | |
| Target area timeframe to lease – 4 weeks excluding units (Property Managers) | Y | N | |
| The area has quality housing control (check council) | Y | N | |
| **Area has accessible amenities** | | | |
| Schools (primary, secondary, and private) | Y | N | |
| Shopping conveniences (local and major retailers) | Y | N | |
| Public transport | Y | N | |
| Parks and local sporting facilities | Y | N | |
| **Value indicators list** | | | |
| New infrastructure | | | |
| Employment generators | | | |
| Roads | | | |
| Shopping centres | | | |
| Private schools | | | |
| Rail | | | |

# Investment property

*Now* it's time to choose your property!

When you start to search for an investment property, you've already knocked out underperforming markets and areas that pose a risk to your strategy. Now you can get specific on the property.

Here are the keys to a smart buy:

- Buy below the median house value
- Make sure the property is low cost to hold
- Optimum size and quality
- Established capital benchmark
- Land content
- Close to amenities
- New over old

# Buy below the median house value

Kids, the key to building wealth is the future bank valuations on the properties in your portfolio. These valuations will dictate when you can duplicate and invest in more property. When picking investments, follow the criteria I've given you. Determine the right market, the best area in that market and then the investment property itself. You must also use your knowledge of the valuation process to maximise your potential for success.

So why is it so important to buy below the established median house value?

There are two reasons. The first is valuation maximisation. When you buy below the median, you have the best chance of a favourable valuation. The second is a low cost to hold. In other words, you can achieve a higher percentage rental yield on the cost of your property.

Keeping in mind that the median house price is the middle value in a series of sales. Be mindful that the median house price of a suburb can fluctuate dramatically if there are lower sales volume.

This diagram shows the importance of buying below the median price.

## Property market & buyer capacity

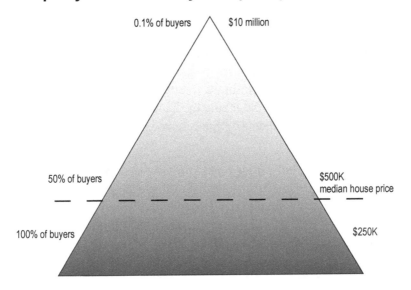

There's only ever a tiny percentage of buyers at the top end. This may mean there are just one or two people at any time who can afford to buy at this level in a particular location. This is why when the economy falters, we sometimes see drops of 20% or more at the top end. If the few top-end buyers hold off, the only way to sell is to drop prices dramatically to attract the next level of buyers. A $10m property may need to fall to $8m before it sells. But this doesn't mean the *whole market* has dropped by 20%. It may not have dropped at all, because the middle sale (the median) is the same.

Look at the diagram again. Think about the median house price and why our target purchase price should be just below it.

Say we buy a $750k house in an area with a median value of $500k. There may be only a few houses in the area that have sold for $650k, and even fewer that have sold for $750k. When we request a valuation, even if the house is actually worth $750k on the market, the valuer will be reluctant to assign a bank valuation at this level. They'll see that the property is above the median and will most likely take a conservative approach by valuing the $750k house at $650k. He'll do this because he knows there's more demand for houses in that area at that price. This isn't ideal when you're trying to build wealth. Conservative valuations are to be expected from bank panel valuers and a 5–10% tolerance level should be adopted. Anything more is a warning something isn't right.

So let's get smart, kids. If we buy a property that meets our criteria of a good investment at a price below the median and we apply the theory that the valuer will check similar house sales and lean towards the median value, we increase the chance of a good valuation and therefore strengthen our overall portfolio value.

When building wealth, buy below the median.

**Low cost to hold.** The more rent you receive as a percentage of purchase cost, the lower your holding costs.

You need to calculate the holding costs of your investments to understand and control your out-of-pocket expenses. This can be done with your accountant, or you can simply set up a spreadsheet where you enter your costs and do the future cost estimates yourself. There are programs you can use if you feel you need something more than a standard spreadsheet. The cost to hold your property will be affected by whether you buy the optimum size for the area you invest in.

Calculation to view your rental yield as a percentage:

Rent = (weekly rent × 52 ÷ purchase price) × 100
e.g. Rent = $450 p/w. Purchase price = $450,000
Yield = (450 × 52 ÷ 450,000) × 100 = 5.2%

# Optimal size – optimal quality

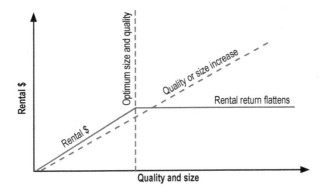

As a home's size or quality increases, there's an optimal point above which your investment doesn't give you an equal return. You can find this point by researching the area to see what kind of property is renting and selling. If you go beyond this point, you won't increase rental yield or, more importantly, the property's value, in line with your costs.

Check that the quality of your chosen property compares with but isn't bigger or better than other family homes in the area. People rent bedrooms. And while most families might like a media room, few pay extra for it. It's much better to invest in a house with an efficient design that maximises the number of income-producing bedrooms without excessive costs, such as building a second storey. Though it's the land that appreciates, a three-bedroom home on a smaller block can give a better rental yield than a four-bedroom home on a larger block, because you're saving on costs.

Here's a simple example of optimal quality. If you find that most properties in your chosen area have vinyl bench tops, and you decide to install stone bench tops, it's likely you'll receive the same rent as the other properties, even though you incurred extra costs.

A more common and costly mistake is failing to understand optimal area size. If you build an investment property 10 m$^2$ larger than the optimal house in an area, you incur substantial additional costs but receive no greater valuation or rental return.

Look online at rentals in a range of suburbs. You'll see that some houses stand out. They may be asking slightly higher rent than the rest because they're bigger or have better fixtures. But they won't rent for much more. Because even though these houses cost a lot more to build, they can only make a rental income in line with the market standard.

There's an optimal size and quality property for every area. Building or buying above this size or quality is a waste of money. Keep this in mind when you do your investment feasibility.

---

**'Dad, how do I do a feasibility?'** If you're building a property, a feasibility is simply adding all your purchase, land and construction costs (including interest during construction) and comparing this to the market to ensure you're under the area's median price.

---

## Established capital benchmark

Kids, when we look at an area's median house price, we also look at its established capital benchmark (i.e. the maximum house price). If it's just 10% higher than your purchase price, you can't expect anything magical to happen. But if you see properties near yours selling for twice what you paid, there's a lot more growth potential. Check that the established capital benchmark is at least 30% above the value of your potential investment. Ensure there were at least three sales in the previous six months at 30% above the price you're looking to pay. You may need to call agents or check rpdata.com (one of the many firms supplying property data and analysis).

## Land content

The total site area must, in most cases, be at least 50% of the total floor area of all buildings. This rules out most apartments and small units.

## Close to amenities

Public transport

< 7 km from a metro train station
< 1 km from local bus route

Education facilities

< 3 km to primary schools
< 5 km to high school
< 10 km to private secondary school/college

Shopping conveniences

< 3 km to local supermarket
< 10 km to major retail centre

Parks

< 400 m from open space

# Housing quality control

Check the future quality of housing in the area, including building design guidelines. Most estates and councils have minimum standards for building construction. Some will be higher than others. If there are reasonable guidelines, you at least know someone can't build a tin shack next to your investment.

# New property over old

Kids, I want to keep this guide as simple and risk-free as possible. That's why I suggest you buy new property. I've bought many older houses and found ways to add value, usually through development. But development has too many risks to be included in a book like this. Maybe *My four-year-old the property developer* will land on my iPad one day!

Here are some of the many reasons I prefer new property over old.

### Maximum tax benefits, including depreciation

Depreciation is an accounting term for a building's general wear and tear. As well as the building, it includes carpets, curtains, taps and fixtures. Depreciation occurs over the life of a building and represents how much it has decreased in value. You can use these losses to reduce taxable income.

### Minimal ongoing maintenance

A new property needs less maintenance to keep it nice. This means less work for you and makes your property more appealing to prospective tenants.

### Builders' construction warranty

Warranties vary by state, but all new homes have a period where you're covered for structural and non-structural issues.

### Tenant appeal

If you had to choose between a fairly new property and one that was 10 years old, which would you rather live in? I'd hazard a guess it'd be the new one, unless the old one was much cheaper (and all you could afford).

# Investment property identification form

| | | | |
|---|---|---|---|
| Investment property address | | | |
| Purchase price (including all costs) (preferably purchase in the lowest 25% of sales) | $ | | |
| Area median house price (RP data, realestate.com.au, API magazine) | $ | | |
| **Top sales in last 6 months** | | | |
| 1. | | $ | |
| 2. | | $ | |
| 3. | | $ | |
| Established capital benchmark | $ | | |
| Rental yield percentage Yield = (weekly rent x 52) / purchase price x 100 = | | % | |
| Optimum size for the area (compare 3 & 4 beds) | Y | N | |
| Optimum quality for the area | Y | N | |
| Land content ratio OK (must be at least 50% of the total floor area of all buildings) | Y | N | |
| New or old—age of house | | | |
| Amenities | | | |
| Public transport < 7 km from a metro train station < 1 km from local bus route | Y | N | |
| Educational facilities < 3 km to primary school < 5 km to high school < 10 km to private secondary school/college | Y | N | |
| Shopping < 3 km from local supermarket < 10 km from major retail centre | Y | N | |
| Parks < 400 m from open space | Y | N | |

Capital growth is determined by what, where and when you buy. Though property will increase in value over the long term, you don't want to acquire property that's going to stagnate for two or three years, if you can avoid it.

Kids, when you follow a set process designed to eliminate the risk of buying a poorly performing investment, you'll soon see that the deal of a lifetime can be found every day of the week.

## Contracts

Put simply, a contract of sale is an agreement that says you swap a sum of money for a block of land, which may have a house. A contract details how the deal is done.

Though contracts can be a foot thick, take the time to read each one. Ask questions until you understand exactly what you're signing. You'll only look stupid if you don't ask questions and sign up for the wrong deal.

Get your conveyancer or solicitor to review contracts and explain them to you before you sign. Ask lots of seemingly silly questions as this is how you learn what to look out for during future purchases.

## Finance

You already have pre-approval from your bank or through your broker. You've chosen your investment, agreed on terms, and all parties have signed the contracts. It's up to you to ensure the finance is formally approved and ready in time for settlement. You need to push everyone and have them agree on deadlines so everything runs smoothly. This finance checklist will help you.

# Finance checklist

| | Y/N or Date | Further action required |
|---|---|---|
| Lender | | |
| Contact | | |
| Contact number | | |
| Email | | |
| Contract date | | |
| Finance approval date | | |
| Contracts posted to:<br>Broker<br>Lender<br>Conveyancer | | |
| Formal approval received from bank | | |
| Approval letter posted to:<br>Broker<br>Conveyancer<br>Builder | | |
| Date settlement due | | |
| Does lender require anything? | | |
| Date loan documents will be ready from bank | | |
| Conveyancer has copies of all signed contracts | | |
| Finance will be available at settlement date | | |
| Settlement date | | |
| Notify builder of settlement | | |

A proficient conveyancer should do all searches for you and stay on top of your broker or bank. Don't rely on them to do this until you've tested them over a number of deals. If you miss your settlement date, you'll have to start paying penalty interest and you could damage your relationship with the seller. Apart from being unprofessional, this relationship may be important in the future, particularly if the seller is a major landholder.

Keep track of everything and check that finance will be formally approved by the date set in the contract. Once you have bank approval, loan documents will be drawn up. Have your solicitor check them over before signing and returning them to the lender.

## Insurance

Have a home buildings insurance policy in place as soon as your finance becomes unconditional. Don't wait for settlement. If the place burns down, you're deemed the future owner and may be forced to settle on the property. I set up policies with the maximum excess as I'm happy to pay $1,000 excess if the property burns down instead of the $300 excess. This lowers the yearly premiums across my portfolios. Factor an extra $20,000 onto the replacement value, as it costs that much at least to clear the site of rubble.

## Settlement

If you're buying an older house, get building and pest checks done before the contract becomes unconditional. Check all the basics before purchase. Ensure doors and windows open and shut, appliances work, floor and rooflines are level, under the house is dry and water pressure is strong. Check the house thoroughly the day before settlement to ensure it's clean and tidy with fixtures and fittings in place. If you're not happy, advise your solicitor to hold settlement until the seller has agreed to compensate you. You can't usually delay settlement if a property is unclean or untidy, but you can have settlement money set aside to cover the costs of bringing it up to scratch.

Your conveyancer will take care of settlement for you and give you an approximate time when it will take place. They'll attend on your behalf and exchange payments for copies of documents to be lodged at the titles office. They should call you shortly after settlement to let you know everything's complete.

Congratulations; you just bought your first property! Now you're an investor, you should be proud of yourself. Time for a few fist pumps in the air.

If you're buying an established house, the agent will hand over the keys. If you're buying land to build, let the builder know settlement has occurred. You'll have already given them a settlement date and they should've told you the date they'll break ground. The sooner they start, the better – as you're now paying interest on your loan.

## Construction

We've discussed some advantages of building over buying an established house. The main one is that you get a property that's the optimal size and quality for your chosen area. When you spend time reviewing plans and building specifications before construction, you can maximise the return on your investment. When you perfect this, you'll be able to create instant equity by minimising unnecessary costs.

If you leave it to a draftsperson, they'll always design a house that's too big. They're proud of their designs and they tend to forget about costs. If you ask an agent, they'll always tell you bigger is better and quality fittings are the go. But remember that agents get paid as a percentage of the sale price, not as a percentage of your return. Agents earn more by selling bigger, more expensive homes, even if you lose money by spending too much on construction! Don't get me wrong; you should add quality investments to your portfolio. Just don't waste money overcapitalising.

Look at every new home for sale or rent in your chosen area, check some out in person and scan the internet to get a clear understanding of the market. Talk to local builders. Ask them, for example, the difference between the sale and rental prices of 170 m$^2$ and 180 m$^2$ three-bedroom homes. While build costs will differ greatly, the sale and rental prices may be very similar.

Ask yourself this. For every thousand dollars I spend, will it increase my bank valuation by a thousand dollars?

## Builder quotes

Once you finalise your plans and specifications, you can ask builders to quote on the same plan and spec list so you can compare prices. When you're deciding on a builder for the first time, the best way to check them out is to talk to at least five recent clients (or even ask to view their houses). Ask them:

- Did the builder start on time?

- Did they finish on time?

- Has the builder responded in a timely way to requests since the house was finished?

- Are they happy with the quality?

- Did they get exactly what they thought they signed up for?

- Would they use the builder again or recommend them to a family member?

Insist on a 'fixed price, no variations' quote and contract so you know what your costs will be to the dollar. Get several quotes and compare every fixture and fitting. I list each builder's inclusions on a basic spreadsheet to compare like with like.

Building contracts usually comprise three parts:

1. Building contract
   The contract details both the builder and your details.

2. Plans
   These must be approved and stamped by a building surveyor.

3. Specifications list
   This details all fixtures and fittings, including size and brand.

A building contract sets out the legal rights and obligations of the builder and consumer. Have your legal team check contracts if you're not familiar with what should be included.

## Plans

When optimising your design, ask builders in the area to look over your plans and give you ideas on how to minimise floor area without reducing expected end value. Builders can be really helpful at this point. It's rare for plans to be drawn to optimal size first time.

## Specifications list

The spec list outlines everything included with your property and breaks down the costs. Ask your builder how to reduce costs without affecting potential end value or rental yield. Don't forget things like grass and landscaping (including plants and sizes), curtains, retaining walls, water tank, driveway, fencing, letterbox, clothes line, security doors, fly screens, air-conditioning and heating. Walk around your own home and check if everything you need is listed. Don't get too excited if a builder offers a free dishwasher or microwave; think of the *overall* build cost.

## Building contract

A building contract sets out the price, progress payments as a percentage and dollar amount, start and completion dates and penalties for missed deadlines. Take note of these items when you review contracts.

Now you've tweaked your plans, created a detailed specifications list and received 'fixed price, no variations' quotes from your prospective builders. When you choose, consider the feedback from the clients you spoke to. The builder due diligence checklist will help you choose well.

# Builder due diligence checklist

| Accountant | | | | | | | |
|---|---|---|---|---|---|---|---|
| Builder's name | | | Contact | | | | |
| Contact number | | | Email | | | | |
| Address | | | | | | | |
| Plan review | Optimum size for area | | | Y | N | | |
| Specification review | Optimum quality (correct specs) | | | Y | N | | |
| Builder's specifications provided | Full specifications list (brands/sizes) | | | Y | N | | |
| Builder's fixed price contract (no variations) | Amount | $ | Extras | $ | GST inc. | Y | N |
| Guaranteed construction time frame | Start | | Finish | | Total weeks | Y | N |
| **Client due diligence questions—complete (x 5 required)** | | | | | | | |
| Start time OK | | | | | | | |
| Finish time OK | | | | | | | |
| Response to issues after completion | | | | | | | |
| Satisfied with quality | | | | | | | |
| Did you get what you paid for? | | | | | | | |
| Would you use the builder again? | | | | | | | |
| Comments | | | | | | | |
| Also get details of property managers in the area who manage properties built by builder. What issues are tenants having? | | | | | | | |

It's now time to sign a contract with your builder of choice. Check that everything in the *quote* is also in the *contract*. When you've signed, you'll need to pay the building deposit (or tell your financier to do so).

Check that your financier has a copy of the builder's contract to complete formal approval. Make sure you know who needs to pay what money and when.

The builder must give you a copy of their insurance document and get the final building permit and stamped plans. Check they have this in hand.

One more thing to note, kids: you need a very close approximation of the cost to build before you sign a land contract, so you can do your feasibility and determine total cost. Remember, you must be very clear on total costs before you can determine your borrowing capacity and you must be sure you're buying below the median house price for the area.

## Construction checklist

There are several construction stages on which progress payments fall due, provided you're happy with the work. A good builder is an asset, so it's worth keeping them on side during construction. As each stage is completed to your satisfaction, make the progress payment promptly. It's the best way to keep a builder happy. The next best way is to bring an armload of beer to the site on the occasional Friday afternoon.

The construction stages are:

1. Deposit—start construction
2. Base—footings and slab
3. Frame
4. Lock up
5. Fix
6. Completion

Have an independent, qualified builder inspect the work and report to you on build quality. If at any stage they find standards aren't satisfactory, tell your builder politely and in writing. Then follow up with them ensure all issues are fixed before further payment.

Certificates and endorsements are required before a tenant can move in.

1. Endorsed and certified plans from council

2. Certification and certificate of compliance for phone, power and water

3. The certified plans and the statement of compliance which need to be lodged by your solicitor

4. Titles must be registered

5. A certificate of occupancy

6. Building insurance

7. A quantity surveyor's report for tax purposes.

Keep your property manager or agent informed of the construction progress so they can find a tenant as close to the completion date as possible.

The house is nearly finished. Let's get a tenant!

## Tenant

I've included a tenant assessment sheet for your property manager. It's far more comprehensive than the one most agents use.

My four-year-old the property investor

# Tenant assessment sheet

| | | | |
|---|---|---|---|
| Property address | | | |
| Number of tenants applying for the property | | | |
| Number of tenants to occupy the property (including children) | | | |
| Age of tenants applying | 18–25 | 26–35 | 36 + |
| Marital status | | Pets | |
| Smokers | | Do they drive a car? | Y   N |
| Approximate proximity of house to their workplace | | Length of tenancy applying for | |
| Forecast rent vs offered rent | | Lease commencement date (target < 2 weeks) | |
| **Employment history (attach payslips)** | | | |
| Current employment (tenant 1) | | | |
| Income | | Length of service | |
| Employer feedback | | | |
| Previous employer | | Length of service | |
| Current employment (tenant 2) | | | |
| Income | | Length of service | |
| Employer feedback | | | |
| Previous employer | | Length of service | |
| **Rental history of tenants (agent reference, rental arrears check)** | | | |
| Agent/landlord feedback | | | |
| Rental arrears | Y   N | If yes, please explain | |
| Inspections feedback | | | |
| Bond returned in full | Y   N | If no, please explain | |
| General comments | | | |

A competent property manager is a great asset, kids. I've tried several. I now use one agency for my properties in Melbourne's east and other agents for properties elsewhere in Melbourne and interstate. Choose an agent at least two months before settlement or construction completion, so they have time to find a good tenant for you. Managing tenants yourself is one of the biggest mistakes investors make. Tenants can be a serious pain in the backside and you don't want your investment portfolio to become a source of trouble.

Your property manager represents you. Call them or leave a message as if you're a prospective tenant. This will show you how polite, efficient and professional they are. Your mum sourced a rental property for us while we built our current home. We were stunned at how unresponsive property managers were. Even though we told them we'd pay a year's rent in advance, we struggled to have our calls returned.

Ask some property managers in the area for their letting, management, advertising and marketing fees. Ask them to list other costs you may incur so you can compare. A professional property manager is worth top dollar if they work with your best interests in mind.

Before you pick a property manager, talk to the agency owner. Ask how many properties they manage. An agency with a solid book (300+) usually has better systems.

It's important to ask the right rent. Even $10 over market rate can add weeks to your tenant search. You must also keep the agent honest. Because their fee doesn't vary much, they may not care if your property rents for $50 below the market rate. But it'll matter to *you*.

If the market rent on your property is $400 per week, it's better to list it at $390 and tenant your property quickly. If you try to get the extra $10, you may have wait a month for the property to lease. And if you lose a month's or even a week's rent, it takes a long time to catch up.

Compare your rental property with others listed in the area and discuss with your agent before deciding on the right price.

You should try to organise the longest lease possible: 12 months is standard. When the lease comes up, check the market and renew it with an appropriate rent increase. Don't let the lease go month to month unless you must. If someone wants a month-to-month lease, it usually means they're about to leave. I increase rent on my properties at every lease renewal. This keeps tenants used to the fact that rents go up.

I've rented to people with kids and pets and had no major trouble. If a property is damaged in any way, the tenants must make it liveable again by paying for repairs or cleaning from their bond. It's your property manager's job to keep the place in order and make sure this happens. That's what you pay them for.

You don't have to spend more money on the property once you have a tenant. As long as it's a good standard for the area, you can be confident in your investment choice. Tenants make all sorts of requests but mostly I refuse. If they *really* want something added to the property, which I believe may add value or future tenant appeal, I sometimes ask them to pay half. If they do, it means they're committed to renting the property long term.

You now have a tenant. Well done, kids; the straight line to wealth is complete!

## Insurance

One thing left to consider is personal insurance. I have disability and life insurance, so if something happens to me, my remaining debt is paid. If you have a family, make sure they'll be provided for.

### Dad's tips

- The fastest way to any point is a straight line.
- Follow each step.
- Use the tools to guide you.
- Identify your investment:
  - the city market.
  - then the area.
  - finally, the property.
- Remember:
  - buy under the median house price.
  - optimal size and quality.
  - low cost to hold.

## The circle of duplication

Great job, kids; you have a property. Whether it's your first purchase or an addition to your portfolio, it's the same process each time. I'm sure it doesn't seem so scary now, since you have a tenant. Especially when you remember that tenant and the government are paying most of your holding costs.

Now the real fun begins. Managing your portfolio is the most important part of your financial freedom strategy. The straight line to wealth is only one part of the circle of duplication – which is a system for managing your portfolio.

---

**'Dad, is the circle of duplication powerful?'** Hell yes! It's even more powerful than when Dad kicks the footy.

---

The circle of duplication is the key to managing and building your portfolio. Its beauty is that it's a lot simpler than the straight line to wealth.

Let's look at the circle and the tools to manage and grow your portfolio.

# Circle of duplication tools & checks

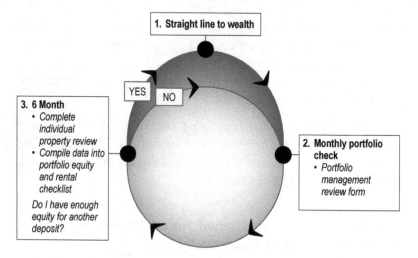

Let's break down the three circle points.

1.  The straight line to wealth lets you identify worthy investments.

2.  A monthly portfolio check helps you to manage your properties, with the portfolio management review form.

3.  A six-monthly equity and rental check determines if you have enough equity to duplicate. Compare sales of similar properties in the area with the property review checklist. Compile the data in the portfolio equity and rental checklist for an overview of your portfolio. This takes a little time at first, but you only do it twice a year. It's not that hard and it's definitely worth the effort.

My four-year-old the property investor

# Portfolio management review form

Insurance: *ABC Insurance*
Policy #: *xxxxxxxxxxx*
Policy expiry: *dd/mm/yyyy*
Agent details: *ABC Agent*
Contact: *xxxxxxxxxxx*
Contact number: *xxxxxxxxxxx*
Last rental review: *dd/mm/yyyy*
Last rent increase: *dd/mm/yyyy $xxxx*
Lease expiry: *dd/mm/yyyy*
Rent due: *Monthly Date:*
Monthly rental: *$xxxx pcm*
QTR/Annual rates: *dd/mm/yyyy $xxxx*

Property: *Address #1*

| 2013–2014 | Jul 2013 | Aug 2013 | Sept 2013 | Oct 2013 | Nov 2013 | Dec 2013 | Jan 2014 | Feb 2014 | Mar 2014 | Apr 2014 | May 2014 | Jun 2014 |
|---|---|---|---|---|---|---|---|---|---|---|---|---|
| Gross rent | | | | | | | | | | | | |
| Expenses | | | | | | | | | | | | |
| Net rent | | | | | | | | | | | | |
| Date banked | | | | | | | | | | | | |
| Amount banked | | | | | | | | | | | | |
| Loan repayment | | | | | | | | | | | | |
| Notes | | | | | | | | | | | | |

# Portfolio equity & rental check

| Date / / | Address | Property description | | Bank valuation | Fair market valuation (Comparable sales) | Current loan amount | LVR | Potential useable equity | Current rent | Market rent | Current / forecast | |
|---|---|---|---|---|---|---|---|---|---|---|---|---|
| | | Beds | Land size | | | | | | | | Interest | Net cashflow |
| Property 1 | | | | | | | | | | | | |
| Property 2 | | | | | | | | | | | | |
| Property 3 | | | | | | | | | | | | |
| Property 4 | | | | | | | | | | | | |
| Property 5 | | | | | | | | | | | | |
| Property 6 | | | | | | | | | | | | |
| Property 7 | | | | | | | | | | | | |
| Property 8 | | | | | | | | | | | | |
| Property 9 | | | | | | | | | | | | |
| Property 10 | | | | | | | | | | | | |
| Property 11 | | | | | | | | | | | | |
| Property 12 | | | | | | | | | | | | |
| Property 13 | | | | | | | | | | | | |
| Property 14 | | | | | | | | | | | | |
| Property 15 | | | | | | | | | | | | |
| Total | | | | | | | | | | | | |

To truly understand market activity, talk to valuers you deal with or ask agents in the area for details of similar property sales. You may also have access to rpdata.com or a similar database.

If you find prices have risen above the current valuations on your portfolio and you have extra equity for another deposit, it's time to give your bank an updated valuation. Again, you'll need to give the valuer sales data to help him reach the valuation level you want. At your request, the bank will increase your line of credit through a loan adjustment or new facility.

Remember that wealth is created when the property valuations across your portfolio increase. Then you can unlock usable equity and use it as the deposit on your next investment purchase.

Never dip into this line of credit or waste it. It should be used for deposits or portfolio holding costs only while you build your initial portfolio.

Set yourself a target before you treat yourself. For example, you might decide to build a portfolio of five properties, wait for a 20% market rise, then spend $50k on family holidays or toys.

When you have enough equity for another deposit, the circle is complete. It's time to return to the straight line to wealth and make another investment purchase.

Kids, I'm happy to say you now have the knowledge, the strategic plan and the tools to build a portfolio of property that'll give you financial freedom.

Remember to follow each step and you'll learn as you go.

## Dad's tips

- Conduct monthly portfolio checks and make sure your rents are paid into your account on time.
- Conduct six-monthly equity and rental checks across your portfolio. If you have enough equity for another deposit, it's time to walk the straight line again.

## Love, Dad

This book is for you, kids.

I'm sure others will benefit from it and I'm cool with that.

I'd like to think I'm laying the foundation and building a house of bricks that'll last for generations.

Of course I need to take into account the three generations rule. The first generation makes it. That's me, good old Dad. The next generation builds on it. That's you. Finally, the third generation blows the lot. That's *your* kids!

But this is only a folk tale and one rule that should be broken. Instead, I want to educate you kids. When Hannah and I go running, after talking about dance moves and which park to stop at, we discuss architecture and what it takes to build a house. I show you kids the plans for houses we're buying for our portfolios and we often look through development plans together. I do this so that over time, you'll become familiar with property and investing.

When you're older, I'll walk each of you through this book. When I buy another property, you can help me chose it by using these criteria. I want you to see how things work, so that before you start building your own portfolios, you'll be familiar with a proven investment system. I'll introduce you to all the different people you need to know and we'll watch the property grow in value together. You'll see how easy it is when you know how to choose and manage the right investments. I'll show you how to leverage a single property and duplicate multiple times.

I reckon by the time you're in your twenties you'll be competent investors armed with expertise far beyond your years. Then it'll be time to start building your own portfolio.

This book is for you. It's also for your kids and their kids. Because if you have an investment manual, something simple enough for a child to follow, I think our house of bricks will stand for many generations to come.

## Dad's famous last words

- Your first few years of investment may seem to move slowly.
- Stay on track and stick to your plan. Always ask yourself: is this part of my strategy?
- Follow the steps in the straight line to wealth when buying. Then monitor the circle of duplication and correctly manage your portfolio until it's time to walk the straight line and buy again.
- Don't waste your equity. Set yourself a target and spoil yourself only when you've earned it by creating a solid portfolio.
- Be humble. You've no one to impress but yourself.
- Follow these steps and you'll be surprised; portfolio growth will sneak up on you. One day you'll realise you're no longer bound by the same rules as everyone else.
- Do what you want, when you want.

Your only limit is your imagination.

Enjoy life, kids.

*Love, Dad.*

**Part four**

# Tools of the trade

## Web link

To access the tools and view educational videos, visit
**opencorp.com.au**

## Straight line to wealth tools and checks

**The idea**

**Setting up your team**
Team members details sheet

**Finance pre-approval**
Pre-approval form

**Identifying the investment**
Market review form
Area review form
Investment property identification form

**Contracts**
If building, complete builders due diligence checklist
Have your legal team check all contracts prior to signing

**Finance**
Finance checksheet

**Settlement**
Conduct a property inspection
Alert your property manager and provide keys
If building, alert builder and confirm start dates

**Construction**
Ensure you engage an independent building inspector to
monitor construction quality

**Tenant**
Have your property manager complete a prospective
tenant checksheet

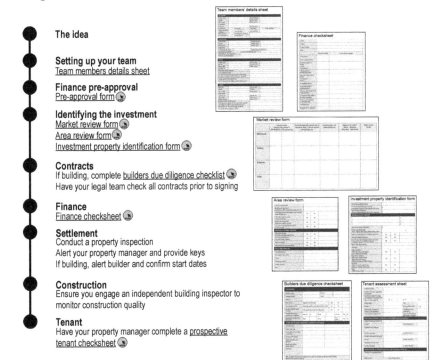

## Circle of duplication tools and checks

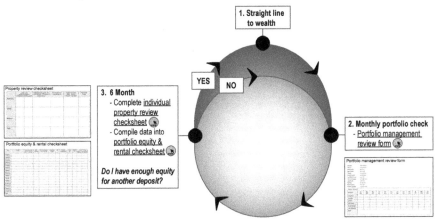

**Part five**

# Glossary/Index

**appointor**
Someone who has the power
to appoint or sack a trustee.
118, 120–1

**assets**
**appreciating** Assets that increase
in value over time. 38, 54, 58–60,
62, 67
**depreciating** Assets that decrease
in value over time. 54, 58–60

**baby boomer**
A member of the generation born
between 1946 and 1964. 132

**beneficiaries**
The people a trust is designed to
benefit. 116, 118–9

**borrowing capacity (BC)**
How much money you can borrow
for a loan. 100, 103, 152, 179

**capital gains tax (CGT)**
Paying a sum of the increased
value of your investment to the
government. 46–7, 49–51, 124–5

**charge, fixed and floating**
A bank can sell the assets of a
company (or person) if they default
on debt payment requirements.
The charge 'floats' until a default
occurs. If the bank exercises the
option, the charge becomes 'fixed'
and the defaulter can no longer
deal or trade those assets.
99, 153

**compound growth/effect**
The exponential increase in the
value of investments. 34, 39–41,
43–4, 69, 78, 81–2, 125

**Consumer Price Index (CPI)**
Measures the change in prices paid
by households (consumers) for
goods and services over time. 28

**contract**
An agreement detailing the swap
of a sum of money for property
or services. 13, 77–8, 99, 112–3,
142–3, 146–7, 150, 152–3, 172–4,
176–9, 195

**cross-securing loans**
When more than one of your
properties is used as security for
a single loan. 96–7, 99–100, 103,
149

**debt service/serviceability ratio (DSR)**
The amount of money you have
available to pay off a loan.
95, 100, 102–3

**depreciation schedule**
A report showing the depreciation
allowances an investor is entitled
to. 126–7

**development**
Making a material change in
the use of buildings or land
(e.g. subdivision), the construction
of a building on land, or both.
11, 13–5, 63–4, 66, 68, 79, 86–8,
123, 157, 161, 170, 190

**directors guarantee**
The directors of a company have
personally guaranteed a loan,
making them liable. 99

**diversified managed fund**
A fund that invests in various
assets to 'spread' the risk. 133

**drawdown**
A payment made to a builder
at each construction stage.
Also known as a progress draw.
13–4, 153

**drip-feeding**
A strategy used by large land
developers. They release blocks
of land slowly to the market to
ensure there's never enough supply
to meet demand, which keeps
upward pressure on prices. 16

**duplication**
Growing wealth through good
investments. 9, 39, 41, 44, 137,
185–6, 191, 195

**employment generator**
An area or location that
provides significant employment
opportunities. 160–3

**equity**
The value of an asset, less the liability or loan held against it. The money you're left with if your asset is sold and the debt repaid. 8, 11, 14, 28, 39–41, 43–4, 47–8, 50, 52, 63, 66, 68, 78–9, 82, 85, 94, 97–100, 103, 109–10, 121, 129, 149, 175, 186, 188–9, 191, 195

**established capital benchmark**
The maximum house price. 164, 169, 171

**exit strategy**
The method by which you pay off your debt. 45–6, 48, 50–1, 61, 100, 122

**feasibility**
When building a property, adding all purchase, land and construction costs (including interest during construction) and comparing this to the market to ensure it is under the area's median price. 64, 86, 161, 168, 179

**financial freedom**
Being free from the cycle of debt. 4, 21–3, 29, 39, 49, 80, 185, 189

**funds management company**
Sources funding from multiple investors, then manages the development process and risk for them. 11, 13

**gearing**
The loan to property value ratio. Low gearing means there's a lower amount of borrowings against a property. 65, 81

**income**
**earned** Income generated through work (e.g. salary or wages). 43, 45, 53, 100, 107–8, 129
**gross** Before-tax dollars. 125
**net** After-tax dollars. 42–3 125, 130

**passive** Income from assets created or bought (e.g. property or business). 28–9, 43, 109
**trading** Income from selling something for more than you paid (e.g. shares or paper assets, real estate trading, buying and selling goods). 108

**infill area**
Vacant land surrounded by established housing. 16, 63

**investor**
**smart** Someone who actively invests in property with a clear vision and a refined system. Contrasted with an 'ordinary' investor. 7, 31, 51, 71–2, 109, 114, 141
**sophisticated** Having enough knowledge to make informed decisions and holding net assets of $2.5m or more, or a gross annual income of $250k or more. Contrasted with an 'unsophisticated' investor. 15

**land content ratio (LCR)**
The size of a property in relation to the land it's on. 56, 171

**lazy equity**
Equity at your disposal but not being used. 39, 44

**legal will**
A document with clear instructions on how your assets are distributed when you pass away. 122

**leverage/leveraging**
Using other people's money (OPM) to give you a far greater return than you'd make on your own. 14–5, 37–8, 68, 81–2, 190

**liability**
**beneficial** An investment that makes money in the long term (e.g. a business loan or phone bill). 58–62

My four-year-old the property investor

non-beneficial An investment
that doesn't make money
(e.g. a personal loan or credit
card). 58–62

loan to value ratio (LVR)
The amount of money you borrow
compared to the property value.
80–1, 94, 100–3, 148–9, 188

market clock
Shows the growth and decline of
the property market. 88

median house price
The middle price in a series of
sales. Commonly confused with
the average sale price (mean or
medium). 33, 35, 95, 164–5, 169,
171, 179, 184

mortgage insurance
A policy a bank takes out to
protect itself on any loan over an
80% LVR (loan to value ratio).
Also known as loan insurance or
lenders mortgage insurance (LMI).
79, 94, 151, 153

negative gearing
When income from an investment
property fails to meet the expenses
of holding it. 121, 128–9

'old money'
Wealth that has been passed down
through generations. 31

OpenCorp
An investment advisory, funds
management and property
development company. 13–6, 75,
86–7, 195

other people's money (OPM)
The money of others that can be
used to make a greater return than
you would have on your own.
15, 37–8, 67–8, 81, 83, 93, 103

pay-as-you-go (PAYG) worker
You or your accountant calculates
your tax refund at the end of the
financial year. 129, 152, 154

portfolio
A collection of investments owned
by individuals, a company or a
trust. 3–4, 7–9, 11–2, 14–6, 22–3,
28, 37, 39–41, 43–4, 46–8, 50,
52–3, 61–8, 74–7, 80, 82, 89, 94,
96–8, 101, 103–4, 109–10, 114,
116, 122, 128–30, 133, 137, 141,
146, 148–9, 156, 164, 166, 174–5,
182, 185–91, 192, 195

prenuptial agreement (prenup)
A contract that determines what
happens to investments if a long-
term relationship ends. 114–5

property flipper
A trader who buys and sells
property in search of short-term
gain. 49

risk matrix
The risk to return ratio. 31–2

risk minimisation
Staying in control by having a
system. 8

self-managed superannuation fund
(SMSF)
A superannuation fund
account that is controlled by
the individual instead of an
institutional fund. 132–3, 150

settlor
To set up a trust, a settlor must
give a small amount of money, to
be held in trust. 118, 120

shark
great white Those who use get-
rich-quick schemes to manipulate
investors into taking risks. 70–1
skimmer Those who charge above
market rates for their services
and/or deliver less than what was
agreed. 70

speculative (spec) home
A home built by a developer who
has designed it by speculating on
the type of buyer or tenant who'd
like to occupy the home. 16, 75

specifications (spec) list
Outlines everything included with your property and breaks down the costs. 176–8

superannuation (super)
The government's mandatory savings plan for Australians, in preparation for retirement. 132–4

trust
An arrangement where property is held 'in trust' (by a trustee) for the benefit of others (the beneficiaries). 3, 14, 47–8, 99, 116–22, 128, 130, 150

trustee
Someone who manages the daily operations of the trust. Can be one or more people, or a company. 116, 118, 120–1

urban growth boundary (UGB)
A limit the government sets to control development growth, dividing urban from regional and high density housing from low. 63

Valex
Distributes valuations to a panel of qualified valuation firms on a lender's behalf. 96, 151

vendor's statement
A document that must be given to you before a contract of sale is signed, containing specific information about the property in question. 146–7

vision
A goal that involves a time, place and an environment in the future that you wish to create. 7, 18, 21, 45

yield (rental)
Money received as rent for a property, usually viewed as a percentage and compared to the property's cost. 3–4, 16, 28, 32, 41–2, 44, 47, 52, 65, 156, 164, 166–7, 171, 177

CPSIA information can be obtained
at www.ICGtesting.com
Printed in the USA
LVHW052328220122
709136LV00008B/367